PREDICTING PERSONALITY

USING AI TO UNDERSTAND PEOPLE AND WIN MORE BUSINESS

DREW D'AGOSTINO & GREG SKLOOT

WILEY

For general information on our other products and services or for technical support, please contact our Customer Care Department within the United States at (800) 762-2974, outside the United States at (317) 572-3993 or fax (317) 572-4002.

Wiley publishes in a variety of print and electronic formats and by print-on-demand. Some material included with standard print versions of this book may not be included in e-books or in print-on-demand. If this book refers to media such as a CD or DVD that is not included in the version you purchased, you may download this material at http://booksupport.wiley .com. For more information about Wiley products, visit www.wiley.com.

Library of Congress Cataloging-in-Publication Data

Names: D'Agostino, Drew, author. | Skloot, Greg, author.
Title: Predicting personality : using AI to understand people and win more
    business / Drew D'Agostino, Greg Skloot.
Description: Hoboken, New Jersey : John Wiley & Sons, Inc., [2020] |
    Includes index.
Identifiers: LCCN 2019040992 (print) | LCCN 2019040993 (ebook) | ISBN
    9781119630999 (hardback) | ISBN 9781119631033 (adobe pdf) | ISBN
    9781119630968 (epub)
Subjects: LCSH: Personality assessment. | Interpersonal communication. |
    Customer relations—Psychological aspects. | Marketing—Psychological
    aspects. | Psychology, Industrial.
Classification: LCC BF698.4 .D34 2020 (print) | LCC BF698.4 (ebook) | DDC
    658.8001/9—dc23
LC record available at https://lccn.loc.gov/2019040992
LC ebook record available at https://lccn.loc.gov/2019040993

Cover Image: Wiley
Cover Design: © temniy/Getty Images

Printed in the United States of America

V10014653_101119

For the Crystal team, who have made it their mission to help others understand each other better, communicate more effectively, and build stronger relationships.

CONTENTS

Contents

PART SIX | PREDICT RESPONSIBLY ———————— **299**

Understanding the proper, ethical use of Personality AI

INTRODUCTION

Since our world has become hyper-connected, it has also become hyper-skeptical. As a result, it is harder than ever to communicate well and build trust with new people.

Most people who need to sell products, convince others to join their team, or drive their audience to take action already know this because their jobs have become harder. As entrepreneurs who spend most of our time talking to, meeting with, and emailing people with specific goals in mind, Greg and I have felt this pain acutely. Throughout our careers, we have repeatedly gotten communication *wrong*, and it has been costly at times:

- We have sent countless outreach emails that never got a response because they weren't compelling enough.

- We have given lengthy pitches that eventually lost the attention of our audience because we didn't focus on the value that they cared most about, nor did we deliver the message in a way that resonated.

- We have let promising opportunities slip away because we didn't follow up with the right approach.

- We have allowed important meetings to get derailed because we didn't manage conflict well.

- We have seen entire companies fall apart because of miscommunication and misunderstanding at the top levels of management.

Some of these communication failures were a result of our ignorance—early in our careers we were often naive about how people thought, behaved, and made decisions. Some of them resulted from our lack of information—we were not always prepared to approach these conversations in the right way or with the right data. Some of them were driven by technology—the sheer abundance of online communication channels can make it almost impossible to cut through the noise.

So, we were faced with the same burning question that most executives, managers, salespeople, marketers, recruiters, and consultants face every day: *"How can we understand people better?"* Our careers depended on finding the answer.

DOUBTING THE USEFULNESS OF PERSONALITY MODELS

As we searched for solutions, we were introduced to personality profiles like *DISC*, which claimed to measure, describe, and even *predict* human behavior. It sounded ridiculous at first, and we were skeptical of these claims. People were too complex. Their behaviors, motivations, and communication styles were too diverse to label with *personality types*. Personality models like *DISC*, *Myers-Briggs Type Indicator (MBTI)*, *Enneagram*, and the *Big Five* were a tiny step away from horoscopes and should not be trusted . . . right?

Well, after a few humbling but fruitful experiences that we will explain later in this book, both of us have learned that the answer is much deeper than that. And it all revolves around *empathy*.

Some of the most successful and recognizable business influencers in the world, like Tony Robbins, Ray Dalio, and Dave Ramsey, have evangelized their own unique philosophies of empathy—taking the time to understand how others think and adapting to them—often with the guidance of a personality model like *DISC*. When we started applying these lessons to our own lives, accepting people as *they are* rather than projecting our own assumptions onto them, we witnessed the incredible power of personality models firsthand.

This was the key insight: when you can accurately measure someone's personality traits, you can understand what they truly care about, and you can use that information to communicate with them more effectively, improve your relationship with them, and earn their trust. With that trust, you gain influence.

JOINING THE PERSONALITY REVOLUTION

When we started using personality profiles for our own management, sales, and recruiting efforts, we loved the way it impacted our conversations, but we quickly ran into a wall. To get an accurate personality profile for someone, we needed them to complete a personality test. That simply was not possible for most of our conversations, so we could not understand the personality types of most of the people we talked to every day.

So, in 2014, we created a new technology to solve that problem.

By combining personality psychology with data science and machine learning, we developed a software product called Crystal that could assess anyone's personality with almost as much accuracy as a personality test, without the actual test. Since its launch, Crystal has helped thousands of companies with millions of personality profiles. These personality profiles help their employees have better interactions with customers, prospects, and job candidates alike.

Our customers are communication-oriented business leaders and professionals who understand how important empathy is for their success, and thus invest heavily in their relationships. Not surprisingly, they are awesome people to be around and they have taught us many lessons that we have applied in our own product and company as we have grown over the years.

We wrote this book for that type of leader, salesperson, recruiter, manager, and consultant, so they have a practical, straightforward guide to this AI-driven personality revolution. If you want to understand how your customers, colleagues, and connections think on a deeper level, these insights can radically transform how you approach every one of your future conversations. When you put personality profiles into practice, you will communicate more effectively, build stronger relationships, win more business, and ultimately thrive in the modern economy.

PART I

The Truth About Personality

Making sense of human behavior in an unpredictable world

Chapter One

THE HIGH COST OF NOT UNDERSTANDING PEOPLE

"The motion has passed."

Click. Beep. Click. Beep.

"The organizer has left the conference."

And just like that, we lost everything.

Greg and I sat in his basement apartment and exhaled. That friendly female robot was gently informing us that our final board meeting was over, and that we had just been fired from the company we started. It was a stinging message delivered with a peppy, upbeat voice.

"Well, what do we do now?" he said.

"Let's just drive."

We needed to get out of Boston. It was early August 2014 and the humidity was thick. After so many months with all-day meetings punctuated by all-night coding sessions, I was feeling claustrophobic, burnt out, and emotionally exhausted.

We hopped into my 2000 Nissan Altima, crumpled up another parking ticket, and started our westbound journey on the Massachusetts Turnpike. It was an odd feeling ... driving in the opposite direction of our office in the middle of a workday. The entire team was back there, going about their ordinary business. Greg's sales team was trying a new go-to-market strategy calling on university advancement offices. My engineering team was cranking away on the new version of our mobile event management app.

The day probably seemed completely normal to them, but they were unaware that they no longer had bosses.

"Where are we going?"

"I don't know. Maybe Cleveland? Chicago? We could just go to California and start something new."

I didn't really care where we ended up. I was numb.

My phone was still buzzing with notifications for website errors and other alerts that I normally needed to attend to as the technical leader. It was now someone else's problem, but it certainly didn't feel that way. I was still CTO in my mind, and I was still debugging, thinking through ways to rearchitect our software in the future.

Greg didn't say much as we drove. This whole thing seemed to hit him more quickly than it hit me, and I understood why. As CEO, he had convinced 30 of the most talented people we could find to quit their jobs and join us in this crazy, risky venture, most of the time with a sharp pay cut. He always felt an intense level of responsibility for our team and their future, and he feared letting them down.

"I'm hungry. Let's just pull off here."

Our getaway lasted about 20 minutes. Normally at this hour we would be perched in our tower—an art deco Fenway office with sweeping views of the Boston skyline. But on this afternoon, a McDonald's booth in the Framingham Service Plaza was good enough.

Over a carton of McNuggets, we recounted the events that brought us here. Back in the spring, everything seemed great. Sales were up, product was moving, demand was growing, and we had a clear path to success. The whole thing started to feel like a real business, and one that could legitimately take off.

But by mid-summer, we were out.

I always thought that our downfall would be some major product bug, or loss of data, or running out of money, or not hitting our sales numbers, or any number of reasons you typically hear about entrepreneurs failing. But it wasn't any of those.

What ultimately did us in was so much simpler and more human than that ... we understood technology, but we did not understand *people*.

FLYING BLIND IN A COMPLICATED WORLD

At the start of 2013, we were a couple of young, ambitious entrepreneurs who followed the startup playbook and tasted some early success. *Build a product, raise venture capital, hire a team, make sales. Code, raise, hire, sell.* The scrappy startup grind rewards immediate, independent action. Collaboration and communication were less important than simply getting things done. It was surprisingly comfortable for us.

However, as soon as the company started to scale beyond the walls of our Mission Hill apartment and we hired the first few employees, we saw both of our jobs change significantly. I had less time to code and spent far more time interviewing, instructing, and coaching. Greg's schedule was dominated by meetings with prospects, partners, customers, and candidates. Without any intentional decision on our parts, our jobs changed from producers to leaders. With almost zero real-world management experience, outside of some university clubs, it was uncharted territory. But, like everything else, we planned to learn on the fly.

And for the most part, we did. Despite plenty of growing pains over that next year, our team expanded, we figured out our business model, and eventually had a real, growing company on our hands. At that point, we began to witness some of the same people-related challenges that most leaders of rapidly growing companies see. Communication needed to be formalized, otherwise details would fall through the cracks. The culture needed to be set up intentionally, otherwise bad habits could take hold. Our hiring process needed structure and standards, rather than pure gut feel.

The stakes were rising, and we did not want to mess this up. We wanted to be *real* leaders instead of imposters with C-level job titles. And we knew we had blind spots—some we were aware of and others that we were not. So, we sought help and hired an executive coach, Walt, who came highly recommended from a fellow founder.

SEEING OTHERS THROUGH THE LENS OF PERSONALITY

Our coach had an impact from Day 1. He had been sitting on corporate boards for longer than we had been alive, and he had several careers worth of experience in strategy, management, sales, and company-building. We brought him our "unsolvable" problems, and while he wouldn't necessarily give us an answer, he could deconstruct it, pick apart the pieces, and show us the reality of whatever we were dealing with so that the solutions became obvious. He was the Yoda to our Luke, and his pool of wisdom was deep.

He also had a superpower—*reading people*.

You could tell Walt about any interpersonal situation in business or life, and with minimal information he could explain exactly what was going on. Like an expert therapist, he could describe underlying dynamics that were at play as if he were sitting in the room. From someone's mere words, he could infer their motivations, their emotions, and even their future reactions.

When Walt talked about people, he peppered his language with a personality model called *DISC*, and he taught us all about it. DISC explains how personality traits often fall together into four different categories:

1. Dominance (D)

2. Influence (I)

3. Steadiness (S)

4. Conscientiousness (C)

Everyone has a *natural DISC type* (behavioral patterns that we are born with and develop as we grow into adulthood) and an *adapted DISC type* (behavioral patterns we learn and adopt from our social or professional environments). Most people display a unique combination of these types, represented by a *primary type* and *secondary type* (for example, a DISC type of *Si* would indicate that *Steadiness* is the primary and *Influence* is the secondary).

If you could identify someone's type, Walt claimed, you could make incredibly accurate assumptions about how they are likely to behave, communicate, and make decisions. Knowing that information, you could vastly improve the depth and effectiveness of every conversation you had.

As an engineer, I was skeptical. People *must* be more complex than that, I thought. Nobody can predict human behavior.

However, the more I watched Walt at work, the more I understood his point. Time and time again, he would make a stunningly accurate assessment about how someone was acting, or what they were saying. These weren't horoscopes. He wasn't making a generalized guess and relying on your confirmation bias to do the legwork. He was identifying patterns of behavior, spread across similar people, and using a standard language to describe those patterns.

We were desperate to improve our soft skills, so we dug in.

We did more research into this idea and discovered a whole world of personality psychology, backed by rigorous studies and research. Some of the world's leading psychologists and neuroscientists discovered that you could, indeed, use someone's observed behavioral tendencies to predict other traits of their personality. Many variables— like brain chemistry, upbringing, and life experiences—can shape someone's personality in a measurable, quantifiable way.

This new way of thinking helped us understand our own behavioral patterns, as they lined up almost perfectly with *DISC*. Giving us even more confidence, we could see these patterns emerge in the people around us, like our family, coworkers, and friends. We had known some of these people for years, and assumed that their different behavioral tendencies made them quirky, or stubborn, or just plain *wrong*.

But understanding the real causes and effects of personality differences showed Greg and I that others weren't wrong; *we* were the ones who were incorrect in our thinking. Many personality traits are as real and differentiating as someone's hair color, but we cannot see them in the same way. For example, someone who is *highly agreeable* may have higher-than-normal activity in their amygdala (the part of their brain that drives many emotions). Unless you're regularly taking MRI scans of your friends' brains, it is impossible for you to see that personality trait visually, even though it is far more important for your relationship than their physical traits.

So, after understanding the personality research and seeing just how wise Walt had become, it was not surprising when he correctly predicted our downfall.

WHAT HAPPENS WHEN PERSONALITIES CLASH ⸻

By 2014, we were spending most of our time in the weeds of building our young company—recruiting people, coding new features, and putting out fires—and we were also learning how to navigate the boardroom for the first time. In a startup, when you raise your first funding round, those investors usually take board seats, which gives them authority over high-level company decisions like raising more money, selling the business, and replacing the management team.

Board meetings can be intense, especially when you are trying to scale quickly with limited information and high expectations. Still, we thrived under the intensity and enjoyed a collaborative, productive relationship with our board in the early days.

We shared some important personality traits with our board, which made things work. In DISC terms, we all had some *D*-type characteristics like being assertive, direct, and competitive. It was comfortable for all of us to be in an environment where we could speak our mind, ask tough questions, and engage in some healthy, respectful confrontation. We also shared a common sense of urgency and industriousness that allowed us to move quickly and place bold bets on ourselves.

However, there were some distinct personality differences at play, which began to reveal themselves more vividly as the company grew. While we were largely blind to them, Walt spotted them almost immediately.

These differences were most apparent at our board meetings. Our investors had expectations for us both to behave in a manner similar to other startup executives they knew, especially for Greg in the CEO role. This included:

- Sticking to the high-level strategies, objectives, and insights.

- Moving quickly and boldly to implement changes.

- Setting aggressive goals and aiming to disrupt large markets.

However, while Greg certainly had his share of *D*-type tendencies as a CEO, he countered them with a lot of *C*-type traits. For example, he tended to:

- Be very detail-oriented and process-driven.

- Pack presentations with lots of data and supplementary information.

- Analyze decisions carefully before taking action.

- Focus on organization and accuracy over speed.

It's easy to see how these two styles can clash—different risk tolerances, standards of quality, and speed expectations. In a particularly *D*-type environment like our boardroom, it's much more important to hammer home the bottom line than get into the details of everything. While Greg assumed that he was doing the *right thing* by being thorough, he didn't realize that his meticulous style was making him less effective.

At the time, we felt the tension, but didn't know how to adapt. Therefore, we kept the same strategy—if only we could get *more* data, *more* accurate projections, *more* pragmatic about our goals, then we could bring back harmony and alignment on the board. However, when Greg continued to communicate in this way, it only chipped away at his ability to credibly communicate with his audience.

Communication was also failing in the opposite direction. Like many cases with results-oriented personalities, our board would often communicate with direct, concise language. Lots of the time, that was an effective style, but sometimes it was difficult for us to completely understand what was going on without more details. Both of us, especially Greg, were comfortable with as much information as possible, and it was stressful to try and read between the lines.

For a while, we worked around these personality differences without being fully aware of them. We were all diplomatic, positive, and future-oriented, which made the board functional in spite of the occasional misunderstanding. However, as soon as we needed to make some bigger, more contentious black-and-white decisions, the underlying issues rose to the surface quickly. Walt described it like this:

"It's all just a game, and you're probably going to lose this one."

What on earth did that mean? We would find out soon enough. With his game analogy, Walt was highlighting the fact that we had some very competitive, autonomy-seeking personalities leading our company with strong differences, but without clear boundaries of decision-making authority. He predicted that this would inevitably lead to a clash.

As I mentioned, *D*-type personalities are sharp, ambitious, persuasive leaders who can command a room and relish big decisions. They are assertive and demand excellence, of themselves and of the people around them. They create a gravitational force of progress wherever they go, driving results forward and moving mountains in pursuit of a goal. They also tend to be competitive and prefer to be in control during tense or unpredictable situations.

In the summer of 2014, our company was at a crossroads, and the board needed to choose what path to take. The management team (us) had some different ideas than our investors about strategy, and it was time to get on the same page.

This is a very normal scenario at a startup—one that can be resolved with a few discussions and compelling arguments. However, by that time our differences had caused so much division that we were incapable of alignment. The pattern was almost like clockwork. Greg would present plans to the board in his normal, meticulously thorough C-type fashion, the board would ask direct, challenging D-type questions, we would dig in our heels, and everyone would leave the meeting a little bit more certain of their own views than before. And those views gradually diverged until they were in different worlds.

"Didn't we do this all by the book?" Greg said as he polished off a McFlurry. "I mean, we built a great team, listened to our customers, built a valuable product. How are we fired?"

Unfortunately, they didn't teach us a whole lot about personalities in business school.

So, even though the business looked promising on the surface, distrust seeped into the boardroom and slowly hollowed out the productive relationship we had all shared at one point. It was as if we spent all our time fixing leaks, replacing windows, and patching the roof. All while we ignored a giant crack in the foundation.

Eventually, Walt was right. Visions clashed, open communication ceased, lines were drawn, and board votes were cast to replace the company's management team.

And that's what brought us here ... sitting on a curb outside a rest stop in Framingham, Massachusetts, unsure which direction on I-90 we wanted to go next. We woke up as startup executives, and by the afternoon we were a pair of confused, unemployed 23-year-olds.

It was at that moment, the low point of each of our careers, where our next mission became clear …

If we were going to figure out this *business* thing, we needed to figure out this *people* thing.

HOW CRYSTAL GOT STARTED

In the months that followed, Greg and I spent a lot of time exploring. Getting ousted from a company is a jarring experience, and it can take a little while to find your feet.

We reflected on our mistakes, wrote up notes for doing it better next time, experimented with a handful of new ideas, explored new technologies, and met with a lot of founders who were pursuing big visions of their own. However, during those months of entrepreneurial purgatory, we kept coming back full circle to that original problem …

How can we understand people better?

Walt had it figured out. His skill for predicting the motivations, intentions, and reactions of people he didn't even know seemed like magic to us. It was magic that we wanted to harness ourselves. We wanted to be like Walt.

We dove deep into psychology, particularly the models and theories that Walt had taught us. Both of us had degrees in business and professional experience in technology, but we were drawn into the scientific study of the human mind and *why* people do what they do.

In this pursuit, we discovered the long-established roots of DISC and other personality models. We learned about cognitive biases and became painfully aware of the blind spots we walked around with every day. We read through the latest research in personality neuroscience, which was progressing rapidly and revealing biological causes of personality traits.

Simultaneously, as the technical side of our duo, I was digging into machine learning and natural language processing. These exploding areas of computer science were making it possible to analyze large amounts of data, find hidden trends, and even *predict the future* in some cases. We saw that these technologies were being applied in such diverse industries as marketing, medicine, sports, law, defense, retail, and more. Wherever there was an abundant set of data, there was an opportunity to revolutionize a market.

Perhaps it was the audacity that comes with knowing *just* enough to be dangerous. Perhaps it was the lack of formal education (but the overwhelming pool of curiosity) in both of these seemingly unrelated fields. Perhaps it was pure wide-eyed, childlike wonder about the pace of technology and the chance to play a part in it.

Whatever the reason, something clicked for us:

What if we could build ourselves a Walt?

At that point, we had some vague ideas for predicting personalities. We hacked away at the problem, building prototypes without much initial success. The goal was to create an algorithm that could come close to reading someone's mind, and we were quickly learning how difficult this would be.

Still, after a few misfires and false positives, we slowly made progress. I remember the first time we saw one of our algorithms accurately predict a personality—we were sitting in my creaky Boston apartment on a weekday, and we felt like we had cracked the nuclear codes.

That algorithm turned into a prototype, the prototype turned into a website, the website turned into a Chrome extension, and the Chrome extension eventually turned into the product that would launch our company, Crystal.

As Crystal grew through its early stages and the technology advanced, I realized that our product captured the imaginations of people in a way that I had never seen before in a software app. We have never made big investments in sales and marketing, but thousands of people kept signing up every week, creating profiles, and sharing the tools with each other. It struck a nerve, and I wanted to find out why.

After years of watching people use it, I've gotten closer to the answer. When people pull up their personality profile for the first time, they start talking about the most important parts of their personality without any prompting, and even if it's our first conversation. I've seen couples who have been married for over 20 years view each other's profiles and start deep conversations that they haven't ever had about their relationship. Crystal gives them a nonconfrontational, impartial third party to open up the line of communication.

That's just the personal side of it. The other day a sales rep named Conrad sent me a message and said, "I have never felt more confident about my emails." A fellow entrepreneur, Marcus, told me that since he started using it, if he goes into a meeting without understanding the other person's personality, he feels like he's flying blind. Large recruiting firms have adopted the technology for their communications with candidates and hiring managers alike.

By introducing such a dramatic shift in how both individuals and organizations can access personality data and an endless number of use cases, we quickly saw that Crystal was not just a new product, but a bellwether of a whole new category: *Personality AI*.

Our customers were pioneers who were buying into a movement—a personality revolution. This movement empowered people with a world of new qualitative information to understand each other much better, and much more quickly than ever before. This book is a guide to this revolution at the intersection of technology, data, and psychology. As Crystal has pioneered Personality AI over the past few years, we have learned a lot of important lessons. In writing this book, we want to share these new insights with every professional communicator who wants to use personality data to do their job better.

Since launching the company, hundreds of thousands of people have joined the platform, without any clever marketing, advertising spend, or a big sales organization. There simply seems to be a huge, growing appetite for personality profiles. We have our theories for this, but the most plausible one is this:

People want personality profiles because they are responding to a *big* problem that lurks beneath the surface of our hyper-connected world. As it has become easier to *connect* with people, it has become really, *really* hard to communicate with them.

Chapter Two

THE INGREDIENTS OF A UNIQUE PERSONALITY

If your job requires you to work with others, build relationships, or lead teams, you're like a chef with a full cabinet of spices. The more you mix them together, the more you discover. Some combinations make you cringe, others make you laugh, and some of them are just *missing* … *something* … that you cannot quite put your finger on.

Like a spice, each one of us brings a unique flavor to the table—our own individual blend of biological traits, formative experiences, and social influences. We call this blend our *personality*.

Scientifically speaking, your personality is a set of behavioral, cognitive, and emotional patterns that make you, *you*. It's the list of words your closest friend would provide if someone asked them, "What is [your name] like?" They might start with your hair color, your height, or your job title, but that's all for context. The real answers are the ones that dwell beneath the surface, like what you care about, what you're motivated by, how you interact with others, and how you see the world. Your external features are a tiny component of *you*, and compared with the internal ones, they are not nearly as interesting.

You're complex. You're unique. You're hard to understand. And you're living in a world with billions of other people who are just as complicated. Life dumps us into a series of melting pots—our family, team, company, and community—that are all packed with cognitive diversity. When the stakes are high, our differences are amplified, and if we don't understand each other, we can encounter a tremendous amount of stress, frustration, and conflict. People have enough trouble understanding their own behavior and thought patterns, let alone others.

Nonetheless, we are social creatures who are constantly interacting with friends, coworkers, and customers who have their own distinct preferences, behavioral patterns, and quirks. Our survival depends on our ability to work together, and that requires us to communicate. To communicate effectively, we need to learn, understand, and adapt to each other.

In our hyper-connected, hyper-skeptical world, that's getting harder and harder to do. People who make their living talking, writing, and meeting with new people feel this pain most acutely as their jobs become more difficult. Ask any leader, salesperson, or recruiter in your network what their biggest challenges are today, and they will likely talk about the obstacles they face with getting through to people and communicating their message.

As entrepreneurs who have a business that *depends* on our ability to build trust with new people, we have been on a journey to solve this problem. Our team at Crystal has spent years combining psychology, technology, and data science to help people understand each other better and communicate more effectively, and this book is an overview of what we have learned so far.

We don't propose to have any silver bullets for 100% email response rates or getting *everyone* to like you. But we do have a set of tools, old and new, that you can start using *today*. Starting with the basics of personality, all the way through communication-enhancing artificial intelligence, we will explain an empathy-driven strategy to understand your audience on a deeper level and start connecting with them in a more genuine fashion.

WHERE DO PERSONALITY DIFFERENCES COME FROM?

With modern personality psychology and neuroscience, we can now attribute personality differences to both genetic and environmental factors. This is commonly known as the "nature versus nurture" theory, and it implies that people develop different behavioral patterns from a mixture of our internal hardwiring ("nature") and external influences ("nurture").

On the nature side, we can observe with near certainty that the human mind is not a blank slate at birth.[1] Variations in our DNA cause some people to have substantially different neurochemistry than others.[2] So, while their brains all have the same systems, those systems can look and behave very differently from one person to the next.

For example, there is a chemical called dopamine that is responsible for your brain's responses to reward and pleasure signals. Researchers have also connected dopamine to several personality traits, including *extraversion*. People with more active dopamine systems tend to be more extraverted than people with less active dopamine systems,[3]

[1] Filip De Fruyt, Robert McCrae, Zsófia Szirmák, and János Nagy, "The Five-factor Personality Inventory as a measure of the Five-factor Model: Belgian, American, and Hungarian Comparisons with the NEO-PI-R," *Assessment* 11, no. 3 (2004): 207–215, https://www.ncbi.nlm.nih.gov/pubmed/15358876.
[2] Timothy Allen and Colin DeYoung, "Personality Neuroscience and the Five Factor Model," *The Oxford Handbook of the Five Factor Model*, ed. Thomas A. Widiger, http://www.oxfordhandbooks.com/view/10.1093/oxfordhb/9780199352487.001.0001/oxfordhb-9780199352487-e-26.
[3] Luke Smillie, Andrew Cooper, Joshua Wilt, and William Revelle, "Do Extraverts Get More Bang for the Buck? Refining the Affective-Reactivity Hypothesis of Extraversion," *Journal of Personality and Social Psychology* 103, no. 2 (2012): 306–326, https://www.ncbi.nlm.nih.gov/pubmed/22582899.

which is actually quite remarkable—it means that there is a segment of the population that is simply born with the tendency to be more social, outgoing, and risk-tolerant.

While it's only one half of the equation, these kind of brain variations help explain the behavioral patterns that seem built-in, and tend to influence a person for their entire life. On the nurture side, however, we can also observe that childhood experiences, social dynamics, and other environmental factors can have both temporary and permanent impacts on personality.[4]

For example, different countries have been found to have distinct trends in personality distribution,[5] implying strong cultural influences on how people think and behave. On a more individual level, family influences like birth order[6] and parenting style[7] can also have a big impact on a child as they grow and develop their adult personality.

While there are undoubtedly personality influences that we have not yet discovered — and even those we are aware of have inaccuracies — we do know one important thing: your personality is not static. The "you" today may not behave like "you" in a few years, as you gradually evolve in the way you process information, experience emotions, and interact with other people.

PERSONALITY DIFFERENCES CREATE PROBLEMS ——

This built-in diversity is a double-edged sword. Our differences make life rich and exciting, but they also create uncertainty, stress, miscommunication, and conflict. In any people-oriented occupation, this is the primary challenge.

[4] Mathew Harris, Caroline Brett, Wendy Johnson, and Ian Deary, "Personality Stability from Age 14 to Age 77 Years," *Psychology and Aging* 31, no. 8 (2016): 862–874, https://www.ncbi.nlm.nih.gov/pmc/articles/PMC5144810.
[5] World Personality Map, https://www.16personalities.com/country-profiles/global/world.
[6] "The Surprising Ways Your Birth Order Affects Your Personality Type," https://www.truity.com/blog/birth-order-and-personality-study.
[7] "How Does Your Parenting Style Affect Your Kids?," *Psychology Today* (blog), October 2, 2014, https://www.psychologytoday.com/us/blog/cutting-edge-leadership/201410/how-does-your-parenting-style-affect-your-kids.

Think about how you have seen personality differences play out in your own career …

> Have you ever seen two well-intentioned people struggle to work together because they just can't seem to get on the same page?

> Have you ever been frustrated with a boss or leader who imposed their own style on everyone else, even when there were clearly more effective ways to do things?

> Have you ever left a job because the role didn't fit with your lifestyle, personal goals, or cultural expectations?

> Have you ever felt like your thoughtfully crafted emails were getting sucked up into a black hole?

There's a common problem at the root of each of these communication failures: people are different and we have trouble understanding others who don't think in the same way we do. And how could we expect anything else? For our entire life, we have seen the world through only one lens. While we all have the ability to empathize with others and find commonalities, it takes an entirely different skill set to accurately understand another person's mental model for how the world works and adapt your communication to earn their trust and make the biggest possible impact on them.

Without the necessary information and skills to understand and adapt to others, we are stuck with a one-dimensional view of our interactions. If we want to build relationships with different types of people and drive them to take action, the best we can do is throw some conversational darts at the wall and hope some of them stick.

Chapter Three

THE BIGGEST CHALLENGES TO SUCCESSFUL COMMUNICATION

We shared that earlier story about our first company not only to explain the origin of Crystal and our journey into Personality AI, but also to illustrate the entire reason this technology exists.

The clash that Walt had identified, between us and our board, was a tale as old as capitalism itself ...

Two parties see a shared goal.

They decide to partner up in their pursuit of the goal.

Something happens to lead one or both sides to stop trusting the other.

Communication disintegrates.

Both parties lose.

This situation certainly was not unique to us. Communication failures come in many different flavors, and while they are not always explosive; they're usually far more subtle and confusing than open conflict.

You may have experienced some of these failures, like:

- The customer who never appears to be satisfied, despite your most valiant efforts to appease them.

- The boss who micromanages your work and won't give you the autonomy you need.

- The prospect who seemed so excited to buy, but has since dropped off the map and will not respond to any of your emails or voicemails.

- The coworker who keeps making promises, but lets the details fall through the cracks while you pick up the slack.

We are software developers by trade, so our successes and failures are usually very clear cut. Does the app run? Yes or No. Does it do what it is supposed to do? Yes or No. Does it crash? Yes or No. If we make a mistake, we can quickly test it, track down the errors, make a fix, write up a note, get yelled at by someone, and then move on to the next problem.

As soon as we stepped into our respective management roles, we realized that *people* were not computer programs. They don't come with an instruction manual. They don't always make logical decisions. They don't always function in the same exact way, even when you think they should. Most of the time, *they* don't even know what they really want to accomplish.

And they especially don't like when you track down their bugs.

The first step to solving communication failures is diagnosing *why* communication has become so difficult in the first place. Some of the challenges are new side effects of the Internet Age; others have been linked to humanity for millennia.

CHALLENGE #1: PEOPLE ARE COMPLEX

As human beings, we are eternally bringing chaos and order to the world around us. The Yin and Yang doesn't just exist *between* people, but *within* people. The conflict seems to be baked into our DNA.

In the field of personality neuroscience, researchers have recently discovered that many personality traits come from observable differences in our brain chemistry.[1] For example, people with above average extraverted traits like *assertiveness* tend to have more active dopamine systems.[2] Additionally, people with highly agreeable traits like *politeness* are associated with higher serotonin function.[3]

These variations can be explained partially by our genetics, our formative experiences, and our social environment. Think about it as your "hardwiring"—the operating system that you base your decisions on, and out of which, your behavioral patterns emerge.

But of course, there's also the problematic mystery of free will that allows us to act in the complete opposite way our hardwiring says we *should*.

[1] Timothy Allen and Colin DeYoung, "Personality Neuroscience and the Five Factor Model," *The Oxford Handbook of the Five Factor Model*, ed. Thomas A. Widiger, http://www. oxfordhandbooks.com/view/10.1093/oxfordhb/9780199352487.001.0001/oxfordhb-9780199352487-e-26.
[2] Colin DeYoung, "The Neuromodulator of Exploration: A Unifying Theory of the Role of Dopamine in Personality," *Frontiers in Human Neuroscience* 7 (2013): 762, https://www.ncbi.nlm.nih.gov/pmc/articles/PMC3827581.
[3] Claus Lamm, Jean Decety, and Tania Singer, "Meta-analytic Evidence for Common and Distinct Neural Networks Associated with Directly Experienced Pain and Empathy for Pain," *Neuroimage* 54, no. 3 (2011): 2492–2502.

When you combine all of this into one person, you get an unimaginably complex stew of emotions, thoughts, and desires. We all have habits, doubts, over-corrections, and external motivations that further complicate things.

And that's just one person. When we work together, we're mixing two or more of those crazy stews into the same bowl and hoping that it tastes good.

In business, bad stew can be very expensive.

CHALLENGE #2: PEOPLE HAVE BIASES

When you spend most of your day working with people, you are navigating a wildly complicated web of alliances, experiences, and personality differences. It's always shifting, always expanding, and always transforming. Right when you think you've made sense of the people around you, they change. Or *you* change. Or you get a whole new group of people to figure out.

The easy response to this relentless social onslaught is to fall back on our personal biases. We start saying things like "there are two types of people in this world ..." or "I only work with people who ..."

The problem with biases is that they become *blind spots*—gaps in your vision that prevent you from seeing opportunities, or even worse, prevent you from spotting danger.

We all have blind spots in our personality. Unfortunately, we often do not even notice them until we crash into something or someone. And even then, we can be too quick to diagnose *someone else's* mistakes rather than our own lack of vision.

Relational blind spots and other kinds of social biases form gradually over time, and we are most vulnerable to them after we've been around the block a few times. Consider the movie *Moneyball*, where the Oakland A's overtake Major League Baseball (MLB) by exploiting the blind spots of the other 29 teams.

Baseball scouting was historically a very qualitative, experience-based skill—much more art than science. When assessing young players to predict their future success, veteran scouts would often say things like "the ball sounds great coming off his bat," or "he has a lot of heart." They also relied on the same traditional statistics that had been used to rate baseball players' performance for over 100 years.

This kind of thinking led to cognitive biases on a massive scale, including:

- *Confirmation Bias:* When we use new information to reinforce our own existing beliefs and ideas, rather than allowing it to influence or change them (e.g. "See? See? I knew this would happen").

- *Bandwagon Effect:* When we rely too much on what other people are doing to influence our decision-making (e.g. "But Mom, EVERYONE is doing it").

- *Halo Effect:* When we assign positive traits to someone or something, based on success in an entirely different area (e.g. "Jill is our best sales rep, so she'll be a great sales manager").

- *Optimism Bias:* When we irrationally believe that we are less likely than others to experience a negative event (e.g. "But that could never happen to me").

Just like personality traits, biases seem to be hardwired into us as humans. They can be useful shortcuts when we want to make decisions with limited information, but they can also lead us to *very* bad decisions if we fail to recognize them. When you're working in a group full of unchecked biases, it's like a whole bunch of cars driving down a four-lane highway with blocked windshields and broken rearview mirrors. You're just asking for a wreck.

Baseball executives were no different—they were just as susceptible to these biases as you and me. As a result, MLB teams were constructed with massive blind spots, and that created an opportunity.

The Oakland A's were one of baseball's poorest teams. They couldn't sign expensive free agents, nor could they throw money at their problems. They simply could not afford to think like everyone else. Billy Beane, their general manager, recognized the rampant blind spots among MLB teams and was the first to take advantage of them.

He disregarded the traditional statistics and relied on the less sexy ones that didn't get as much attention—but they had much more of an impact on winning games. He bucked against the gut-driven scouting approach in his own organization and implemented a much more systematic, analytical one. He ignored the *big name, big money* free agents on the market and instead signed players who had hidden, untapped potential.

He worked under the radar, squarely in the blind spots of his competitors, and the results were revolutionary.

With a less biased, data-driven approach, the 2002 Oakland A's finished with the 2nd best record in the league, winning the division, and at one point winning 20 straight games. Their strategy (coined as "moneyball") was soon adopted by more teams, and it quickly changed the way baseball teams viewed their players.

When we walk around with our biases unchecked, our blind spots can grow. We miss opportunities, make mistakes, and leave ourselves vulnerable to competition. We fail to connect with our customers, frustrate our colleagues, and disappoint our loved ones.

Therefore, we need to be methodical, even surgical, about finding our blind spots. At Crystal, we call this *dragging our flaws into the light*. We can't make progress without it.

CHALLENGE #3: PEOPLE ARE INCREASINGLY SKEPTICAL OF EACH OTHER

Humans have a deep, transcendent desire to *know* and *be known*. We're built for connection and we only survive in communities.

The Little Mermaid said it best … "I want to be where the people are." So it's no surprise that we're all addicted to our smartphones.

For better or for worse, social media takes full advantage of that impulse and gives us unprecedented access to relationships, or at least, the illusion of relationships. By making "connection" and "communication" so easy, it has introduced some subtle, but profound, dynamics to our collective psyche that we are still figuring out:

- *We have more control over how others perceive us.*

  I can carefully craft my public profiles into a specific, strategic persona, whether or not that persona reflects who I am as a person. I can thoughtfully curate the parts of my life I want you to see, and I can omit the less flattering parts.

- *We view relationships more like a checkbox.*

  Connecting on LinkedIn or becoming friends on Facebook *should* be the first step in a new relationship, but it's often the last. How many people have you met once and never really spoken to again, while you passively watch their life from a distance through the feed?

  I can name more than a handful of people to whom I am more of a *fan* than a *friend*, and if I saw them in person I'd probably be embarrassed to share how much I knew about their last vacation. We might not even make eye contact. But hey, we're Friends.™

- *We have "infinite" options of people.*

  In economics, when you increase the supply of a good in a market, the price goes down. In a sense, we have all made ourselves available on the "market" of these social networks— what happens to the value of each relationship if the number of potential new relationships is infinite? How do we treat each other differently as a result?

You can see these dynamics playing out in real time, across professional life, friendships, dating, and every other dimension of our social world. This Golden Age of *communication technology* may be creating a Dark Age of *communication*, as we struggle to recreate the authenticity of face-to-face relationships with screens, bits, and wires.

Communication professionals in sales, recruiting, and leadership positions can feel this shift sharply, as their jobs get harder and harder. While they are judged on their ability to set up meetings, have meaningful conversations, and build long-term business relationships, their prospects are playing defense by default.

And who can blame them? Their inboxes are overflowing from automated emails, and they can't differentiate the ones sent by humans from those sent by the robots. They get random connection requests all day from yet *another* person with a boilerplate explanation of how they can solve all of their problems, if only they can have "15 minutes on the calendar sometime this week."

How can one expect to get a response in that kind of environment? Even the most likeable, credible, and authoritative professionals can struggle to connect.

Chapter Four

HOW TO UNDERSTAND ANYONE'S PERSONALITY

Where was the last new place you traveled to?

For me, it was Italy. I recently took a road trip from Sicily to Rome on an Ancestry.com-fueled adventure to discover my family roots.

While you cannot have a much more Italian last name than "D'Agostino," I speak almost zero Italian, had never been to the country, and did not know much more about my heritage than the typical slightly-above-casual *Godfather* fan. Sure, I had access to plenty of information. Wikipedia could tell me about the Romans. TripAdvisor could tell me where to find Pompeii. Yelp could show me a thousand gelato shops in Palermo.

However, knowing some *facts* about a place is not the same as *knowing* the place.

After a year of reading articles about Roman history, I still would not be able to tell you what it feels like to stand in the middle of the Colosseum and imagine life as a gladiator. TripAdvisor did not tell me what it feels like to watch the sun set on Mount Vesuvius. Yelp, unfortunately, could not tell me what streetside gelato tastes like on a humid Sicilian evening. To get all of that, to *know* the place, I needed to visit.

People are similar. With as little as a social profile, I can learn lots of things *about* you without ever meeting you. I can probably find out where you have worked, where you went to school, who your friends are, and how you decided to dress up your dog for Halloween. In most cases, I can even get some more qualitative insights, like your interests and preferred political causes.

But does that mean I *know* you? Certainly not. There's far more to you than meets the eye, and way more beneath the surface of your thoroughly manicured LinkedIn profile.

You have goals you're working toward and deep motivations that keep you moving. You have a unique voice, a well-developed writing style, and ways that you prefer to consume information. You have habits, fears, pet peeves, and core values that only your close friends know about. You have *character traits* that are just as real as your hair color, or your height, but they are invisible to someone who doesn't know you.

Like an iceberg, there's only a small part of you that sits above the surface for all to see. The part beneath is much bigger, more mysterious, and ultimately more important. The world may know you as a vice president of finance at a Fortune 500 company with an MBA from Harvard, but your family may know you as "supportive, analytical, fiercely loyal, and a little bit stubborn about pizza."

As someone in a job that requires you to build trusting, sincere relationships with people, wouldn't it be amazing to have this kind of information for everyone with whom you came into contact? Of course, there are obvious limitations here because you are human. You only have so much time, energy, and Starbucks gift cards at your disposal to get to know your prospects, clients, and colleagues.

But what if you could get a little bit closer to knowing the important things—like someone's motivations, temperament, and perception of risk? If you had access to that kind of information, how would it change the way you communicate?

That's where personality models come in. For thousands of years, philosophers and psychologists have observed differences in human behavior and created various structures to represent each type. Personality tests have always been a reliable method for detecting someone's personality type, and they have continued to improve in recent years.

However, personality tests can be difficult or impossible to administer. What about the millions of people who I don't know, and therefore cannot ask to take a personality test? Am I simply limited to know about the personalities of my immediate network and a few famous people?

That's where big data, artificial intelligence, and modern psychology research have converged to enable a brand new category of information that can help people understand each other better and communicate more effectively than ever before. It's called Personality AI.

THE EMPATHY EQUATION: A FORMULA FOR SUCCESSFUL INTERACTIONS

Everyone has a unique mental model of the world—an idea of how reality works, which determines how they interact with others, what they expect from others, and how they make decisions.

Your ways of thinking may differ dramatically from the people you work with, sell to, or buy from. Combined with diverse backgrounds, social expectations, and behavioral tendencies, it can sometimes make it very hard to communicate.

However, it's not impossible. It can be helpful to break down tough problems to their building blocks. In this case, we want to define the most important ingredients of an interaction as a formula, and then create a standard approach that we can apply to every interaction in the future.

We have an approach to this called the *Empathy Equation*:

What + Why + How

The equation is a simple way to set yourself up for the greatest chance of success in every meeting, call, or email. It requires you to identify three key things before you interact with someone:

1. *What* they want from the interaction.

2. *Why* they want it.

3. *How* they want to interact.

For example, if I'm preparing to ask my boss for a raise, it's going to be a high pressure, nerve-wracking meeting. I can't trust that I'll be particularly bold or quick-witted in that meeting, but if I can fill in the Empathy Equation beforehand, I can go in much more confident that I'll get the result I'm looking for:

- *What* = My boss wants me to be productive, motivated, and committed to our company for at least the next two years.

- *Why* = If the team exceeds our annual targets and retains its top performers, my boss is in line for a big promotion.

- *How* = My boss is most comfortable with lots of historical data and logic to support decisions, so I should prepare as much external research as possible before our meeting.

Or, let's say I'm selling event management software and I'm struggling to get in touch with the event organizer at a large university. Before I send my next email, I should do the same mental exercise:

- *What* = The event organizer wants to get as many successful alumni as possible to register for this year's big events.

- *Why* = With high alumni attendance, the university can hit its fundraising goals and the events department will get more attention and a larger budget from the board.

- *How* = This particular event organizer is extremely direct and action-oriented, so I should keep my email very brief and avoid overly formal language.

Simple strategies usually run circles around complicated ones, and with so many conversations every day, it's important to boil them down to the essential components. Understanding the what, why, and how underlying every conversation gives you a foundation to build from, a map to follow, and a net to fall back on in case the conversation goes sideways.

When you work with someone every day, you can ask questions over time and learn about their *what*, *why*, and *how*. However, when you're initiating conversation with someone new, or you encounter a difficult situation, these answers aren't always clear, and you don't have a lot of time to find them.

Personality theory helps us make sense of this information quickly, and in a structured way.

THE BASICS OF PERSONALITY PROFILES

If the Empathy Equation is the engine for understanding and connecting with anyone, personality information is the fuel.

Knowing someone's *decision-making process* can tell you a lot about *what* they want.

Knowing someone's *core motivations* helps you understand *why* they want it.

Knowing someone's *communication style* tells you *how* to personalize your message in a way that captures their attention and drives them to action.

Of course, this information usually takes some work to uncover. Even if you're working closely with someone, you may not have enough insight into their personality to anticipate how they will behave in a new situation.

For more than 2000 years, philosophers, psychologists, and now data scientists have attempted to build models to understand personality variations, and the resulting patterns of behavior. Their work spans across many disciplines and their insights have emerged from clinical observation, theology, academic research, and most recently, from analysis of large datasets.

While methodologies have changed over time, the goal has remained consistent—to understand if personality types truly exist, and if so, how they differ from each other.

QUICK OVERVIEW OF THE MOST POPULAR PERSONALITY MODELS

People are never 100% predictable, but they are also not totally random in their behavior. We follow patterns, and many seemingly unlinked behaviors are actually clustered together with others across the population. *Personality models* help us describe these behavior patterns.

You may have heard of some of the more popular personality models, like the Myers-Briggs Type Indicator, DISC, Enneagram, or the Big Five. These models all explain behavioral variations with a standard set of personality *types* or *traits*, and some are more scientifically proven than others. Each has its own strengths and weaknesses, and they can be applied in different situations.

While no personality model is a perfect formula for predicting behavior, one of the most valuable things a model gives us is the ability to speak with a common language about behavior in an objective, nonjudgmental way. Speaking about someone's behavioral tendencies in terms of neutral, quantitative traits is far less personal than anecdotal one-on-one feedback, and it makes personality-focused discussions far more productive, nonconfrontational, and enjoyable. As you become familiar with a personality model, it can help inform your approach for conversations and relationships every day.

The following pages include a brief overview of each of the major personality models (Table 4.1 at the end of the chapter provides a side-by-side comparison).

Big Five

The Five Factor Model, more commonly known as the Big Five, is the most scientifically validated personality model and the one most commonly used for psychology studies.

Psychologists have identified five independent traits that do not correlate with each other across any population, each trait with its own causes and observable behaviors:

1. Openness

2. Conscientiousness

3. Extraversion

4. Agreeableness

5. Neuroticism

Each trait is represented by a percentile against the general population. For example, I have higher *Openness* than 91% of the population, but higher *Conscientiousness* than only 45% of the population. While this precise trait measurement makes the Big Five extremely reliable, accurate, and useful for the study of individuals, it is not as useful for application in relationships, communication, and business.

Myers-Briggs

The Myers-Briggs Type Indicator (MBTI) is perhaps the most well-known personality assessment. The creators, Katharine Cook Briggs and her daughter Isabel Briggs Myers, originally based their work on the *psychological types* of Carl Jung.

The model has four "dichotomies" that represent differences between people on a specific dimension of personality:

1. Introversion (I) and Extraversion (E)

2. Intuition (N) and Sensing (S)

3. Feeling (F) and Thinking (T)

4. Perception (P) and Judging (J)

The MBTI was developed from clinical observation, rather than controlled research. While the model is very popular and has helped fuel the rise in general public awareness of personality types, it has been criticized for several notable flaws, including:

• Each personality trait is represented as a binary "either or," rather than a normal distribution (i.e. a bell curve), which is how traits are actually spread across a population.

- There is evidence that some of the trait differences are actually not mutually exclusive.[1]

Despite the criticism, the MBTI can still be helpful for initiating conversations about personality differences and understanding behavioral variation at a high level.

Enneagram

The Enneagram is a personality model with roots going back more than a thousand years, but it has recently exploded in popularity. The model consists of nine main types, and it attempts to describe deep motivations, fears, and emotional drivers behind our actions rather than purely identifying behavioral traits. Since it lacks the level of empirical evidence and rigor of the Big Five model, the Enneagram is not used as frequently for the scientific study of personality. However, it is often used in self-development, counseling, and relationship coaching.

DISC

DISC is a "four-factor" personality model that was developed in the early 1900s by psychologist William Marston, who also happened to create Wonder Woman and the polygraph.[2] It closely resembles other four-factor models that have been around for more than 2,000 years, ever since Hippocrates described the "four temperaments."[3]

---

[1] Richard Lippa, "Gender-Related Individual Differences and the Structure of Vocational Interests: The Importance of the People–Things Dimension." *Journal of Personality and Social Psychology* 74, no. 4 (1998): 996–1009.
[2] A Biography of William Marston, Creator of Wonder Woman (Web Exclusive, Extended Version) https://www.marintheatre.org/productions/lasso/lasso-of-truth-marston-bio.
[3] D. W. Ekstrand, "The Four Human Temperaments," The Transformed Soul, http://www.thetransformedsoul.com/additional-studies/miscellaneous-studies/the-four-human-temperaments.

The model observes four primary behavioral patterns that are evenly spread among the population. Each pattern has a set of characteristics that are often clustered together, even though they may seem unrelated:

1. Dominance (D)

2. Influence (I)

3. Steadiness (S)

4. Conscientiousness (C)

Four-factor models of personality emerged out of clinical observation but have also been validated by scientific research. Studies have shown correlations between four- and five-factor personality models,[4] specifically along the traits of Conscientiousness, Extraversion, and Agreeableness.

The simplicity and accuracy of DISC has made it very popular in the professional world among coaches, consultants, and trainers. It is most useful in situations where utility, application, and interpersonal behavior change is most important, such as sales, marketing, leadership, and talent development.

[4] C. S. Jones and N. T. Hartley, "Comparing Correlations Between Four-Quadrant and Five-Factor Personality Assessments," *American Journal of Business Education (AJBE)* 6, no. 4 (2013): 459.

Table 4.1 Summary of the major personality models.

MODEL	BENEFITS	CRITICISMS	BEST USE
Big Five	• Most scientific validity and reliability. • Frequently used in psychology studies. • Very precise measurements for individual traits.	• Difficult to draw general insights and advice. • Trait Neuroticism tied to many negative social outcomes.	• Individual personality assessments. • Population-level personality studies. • Counseling and therapy.
Myers–Briggs Type Indicator (MBTI)	• Most popular among the general public. • Easy to understand. • Many online resources for learning.	• Overly binary traits (one or the other, without in-between). • Certain traits lack strong validity.	• Personality discussions with a wide audience. • Self-development programs.

Table 4.1 (continued)

MODEL	BENEFITS	CRITICISMS	BEST USE
DISC	• Easy to learn. • Useful for both individual and relational insights. • Popular among professional coaches and consultants.	• Very general insights in its simplest form. • Insights focus on behavior, rather than deeper thought patterns.	• Professional coaching and training. • Improving communication and relationships. • Career and lifestyle decisions. • Team-building and leadership development.
Enneagram	• Rapidly growing in popularity. • Describes deep motivations, fears, and emotional drivers.	• Lack of rigorous validity and reliability studies. • Tends to be more subjective and susceptible to personal biases.	• Individual self-help and counseling. • Relationship coaching.

Chapter Five

THE PERSONALITY MAP

At Crystal, we have adopted DISC as our primary model for a few reasons:

- *It has stood the test of time:* DISC itself is a modern adaptation of the Four Factor Model, which is over 2,000 years old.

- *It is scientifically valid:* DISC has been linked[1] to the Big Five traits, which is the most commonly used personality framework in psychology research. While the Big Five model is useful for study of an individual's personality against a population, DISC is more useful for explaining communication and relationships between people.

- *It is flexible, but easy to understand:* DISC only requires you to remember four main behavioral patterns, but those four types can combine and break down in many combinations. It's easy for anyone to grasp in a few minutes.

[1] Cathleen S. Jones and Nell T. Hartley, "Comparing Correlations between Four-Quadrant and Five-Factor Personality Assessments," *American Journal of Business Education* 6, no. 4 (July 2013): 459–470.

With a combination of existing research and millions of personality data points collected from Crystal users, we have identified 16 different behavioral patterns that people tend to fall into. We call these *archetypes*.

Each archetype has a name to loosely describe the associated behavior, and each one is associated with a DISC type. These are listed in Table 5.1.

Table 5.1 DISC type, archetype, and associated traits.

ARCHETYPE	DISC TYPE	COMMON TRAITS
The Captain	D	Assertive, Direct, Persuasive
The Driver	Di	Persuasive, Spontaneous, Confident
The Initiator	DI	Confident, Risk-Tolerant, Adventurous
The Influencer	Id	Adventurous, Visionary, Enthusiastic
The Motivator	I	Enthusiastic, Open, Flexible
The Encourager	Is	Flexible, Inviting, Outgoing
The Harmonizer	IS	Outgoing, Peaceful, Warm
The Counselor	Si	Warm, Diplomatic, Supporting
The Supporter	S	Supporting, Nonconfrontational, Consistent
The Planner	Sc	Consistent, Deliberate, Risk-Averse
The Stabilizer	SC	Risk-averse, Structured, Detail-Oriented

(*continued*)

Table 5.1 (*continued*)

ARCHETYPE	DISC TYPE	COMMON TRAITS
The Editor	Cs	Detail-Oriented, Meticulous, Analytical
The Analyst	C	Analytical, Formal, Objective
The Skeptic	Cd	Objective, Logical, Methodical
The Questioner	CD	Methodical, Inquisitive, Rigid
The Architect	Dc	Rigid, Persistent, Assertive

To use DISC effectively, you don't need to memorize the types. Instead, we created a visual reference called the *Personality Map* (see Figure 5.1).

The Personality Map is a visual representation of DISC, with each archetype positioned on top of its corresponding DISC type.

WHERE YOU FALL ON THE PERSONALITY MAP

Everyone has a natural position on the Personality Map (which can be represented by a single dot), and that position falls within one of the 16 archetypes. For example, my dot falls inside the *Influencer* archetype, as you can see in Figure 5.2.

My personality archetype *does not* explain or predict my personality in every situation. I'm way too random for that to be true. However, my archetype does describe *how much* or *how little* energy it takes for me to behave in certain ways.

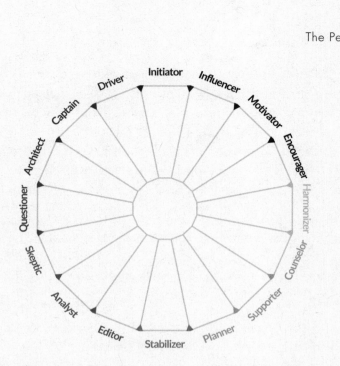

Figure 5.1 The Personality Map with 16 unique personality types.

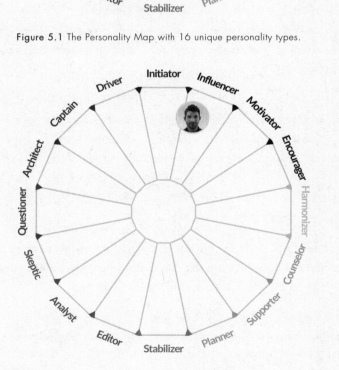

Figure 5.2 Drew's position on the Personality Map.

Every behavior has a position on the map as well, closest to the archetype that most naturally exhibits the behavior. For example, "teaching a colleague a new skill" requires lots of personal interaction and patience, so it falls on the far right side of the Personality Map along with the *Counselor*, *Supporter*, and *Planner* archetypes. On the other hand, "improving a system to make it more efficient" requires lots of deep, independent, logical thinking and sits on the far left side of the map.

Think about your position on the Personality Map as your "behavioral home." If a behavior is close to your home on the map, it doesn't take much fuel to drive there. You can go there all day and still have a full tank.

However, if a behavior is far away from your home on the map, it's going to take much more fuel to get there. Sure, you can drive across the map sometimes, but if you keep going there over and over again, eventually you're going to run out of gas. And that's not good for anyone.

As a natural *Influencer*, it's very easy for me to behave in ways that are typically associated with the *I DISC type*, and some of the ways that are associated with the *D DISC type*. Some examples would be speaking in front of groups or leading a team through a chaotic situation. However, other activities that may be easy for other people— like working with spreadsheets or planning an event—actually drain my energy very quickly (see Figure 5.3).

Of course, I am perfectly capable of planning an event or working in Excel. But the map tells me that those activities are very far away from my home, so they are likely to take a lot of energy.

As you can imagine, this has big implications for the job you choose, the people you choose to work with, and the way you choose to structure your life. We will discuss that later, but first let's dive into the map itself to understand what your position actually means …

Figure 5.3 Each position on the Personality Map has activities that come naturally.

VERTICAL POSITION: HOW YOU INTERACT WITH YOUR ENVIRONMENT

Your vertical distance from the center of the map, top to bottom, tells us how you generally prefer to interact with your physical and social environment (see Figure 5.4).

Archetypes on the top half of the Personality Map tend to direct, shape, and change the environment around them. With a higher position on the map, you are likely to be more comfortable with control over your surroundings. You are also likely to have a high tolerance for risk and unpredictability.

Archetypes on the bottom half of the Personality Map, however, tend to organize, stabilize, and bring structure to their environment. With a lower position on the map, you may be more risk-averse and detail-oriented, often comfortable when someone else chooses the direction while you make sure everything runs smoothly.

**Directs, shapes, and
changes the environment**

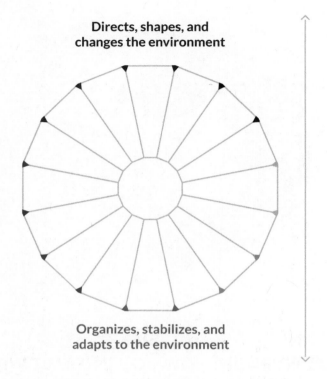

**Organizes, stabilizes, and
adapts to the environment**

Figure 5.4 The Personality Map showing top to bottom differences.

HORIZONTAL POSITION: HOW YOU INTERACT WITH OTHER PEOPLE

Your horizontal distance from the center of the map, left to right, tells us how you naturally interact and collaborate with other people (see Figure 5.5).

Archetypes on the left side of the Personality Map tend to act more independently and value autonomy. They often maintain some distance and skepticism early on in relationships until mutual trust has been established, and they typically communicate with more formal, business-like language.

Archetypes on the right side of the Personality Map usually have an opposite approach to new relationships, as they tend to be more open and trust people by default. They also tend to communicate with warmer, more casual language.

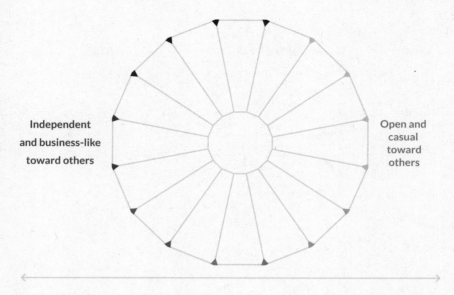

Independent
and business-like
toward others

Open and
casual
toward
others

Figure 5.5 The Personality Map showing left to right differences.

NAVIGATING A COMPLEX, BIASED, HYPER-CONNECTED WORLD

With all of these personality differences, our built-in biases, and overwhelming noise, the modern economy can be an intimidating place to work. It may feel like the communication game has changed forever.

But when you dig a little bit deeper than the new communication channels and networks, the rules are still the same. People are still people. We still have the same wiring, the same core desires, and we follow the same behavioral patterns that we always have. The truths about human nature and personality are just as rigid and unchanging as the laws of physics.

We're still playing the same game, but on a very different field. If we want to succeed as professional communicators, we must adapt our strategy. In the following chapters, you will learn how to identify and harness your own personality type, how to understand the personality types of others, and how to use that information to be more successful in your career.

PART II

Read Your Own User Manual

Understanding your personality and how to harness it

Chapter Six

PERSONALITY DIFFERENCES SHAPE EVERY RELATIONSHIP

"Here ... FISHY FISHY FISHY!!!"

Thanks to Ernie, millions of eager children have yelled that exact call from boats around the world.

Watching that famous *Sesame Street* clip[1] as an adult, you empathize with Bert. He is supposedly the more studious, knowledgeable half of the duo—he has a favorite book called *Boring Stories* and collects paper clips—but his logical, tried-and-true fishing methods do not yield any results. While he patiently sits with rod, reel, and sinker, following the traditional rules without any success, it seems ridiculous—almost unfair—that Ernie's silly fish call works so well.

"Three fish ... Four fish ... Five fish ..."

To Bert's surprise, the fish leap into their boat, one after the other. His skepticism quickly turns into curiosity and he asks his more

[1] "Sesame Street: Bert and Ernie Fish Call," *Sesame Street*, https://www.youtube.com/watch?v=cUusX1Js6RO.

extroverted friend for advice. While the whole thing seems crazy, Bert is a pragmatist and when he sees a strategy that works, he can be convinced to change. Ernie gives him simple instructions and Bert tries a call of his own, but to no effect.

"Bert, that's not loud enough. You're calling very quietly."

Bert tries again.

"Still not loud enough."

For the outgoing, fun-loving, optimistic Ernie, the fish call comes naturally. He lets it out like a song, straight from his heart. But despite Bert's repeated attempts, this odd behavior seems out of place. He is a serious character with lots of self-control, and you hear the hesitation in his voice. The call feels forced.

Eventually, Bert belts out a mighty, awkward fish scream. Finally, *something* jumps into the boat … a shark. He turns at the camera and gives the audience his signature "not again" face, and then faints (much to Ernie's amusement).

With their wildly contrasting personalities, this dynamic has played itself out in hundreds of situations on *Sesame Street*, captivating entire generations of young viewers with conflict, confusion, and reconciliation. These two characters *should not like each other*, yet they have built a loyal, trusting friendship that has lasted for decades. While they live in a fictional puppet world designed for children, the relationship between Bert and Ernie reveals a deep, enduring truth about human beings that we can all learn from.

People are wired in different ways, and that makes the world endlessly fascinating. It also makes things very messy.

Billionaire investor Ray Dalio[2] recognized this fact in his book, *Principles*, and described the "great brain battles" that take place within every individual as they try to make sense of reality. Thinking

[2] Ray Dalio, Founder and Co-Chief Investment Officer, Bridgewater Associates, https://www.forbes.com/profile/ray-dalio/#19100df5663a.

vs. feeling, planning vs. perceiving, left brain vs. right brain, focusing on tasks vs. focusing on goals—each one of us is programmed with a unique set of these psychological characteristics.

Our particular set of attributes, or our personality, is like an operating system that causes each of us to interact with the world in different ways. When one person's system tells them *danger*, another person's system may see the same exact thing and say *opportunity*. One person may see a crowd of people and retreat, while another person may see the same crowd and approach with curiosity. You can probably describe, with painful specificity, how these differences exist in your own family.

Why is that? How are we all so similar, but at the same time, *so different*?

For thousands of years, philosophers, psychologists, and neuroscientists alike have all asked that question. Diversity seems to be built into civilization. When we harness our differences, we can pursue amazing accomplishments and achieve balance, harmony, and progress. When we let our differences divide us, we are capable of incredible destruction and never-ending conflict.

Today, personality psychology is still far from an exact science. We are, however, beginning to unlock some of the complexities within the human mind to understand *how* people behave, *why* they behave in that way, and *what* causes those patterns. Scientific research, clinical observation, and real-world experience has taught us that while it is impossible to predict behavior with 100% accuracy, it *is* possible to understand how someone is *likely* to behave in a given situation with a reasonable level of confidence.

At his company, Dalio uses this key principle[3] (he refers to it as, "Understand that people are wired very differently") to communicate effectively, build team chemistry, and set his people up for success. His advice for other entrepreneurs, leaders, and professionals is simple: Find out what you and others are like, and use that information to manage yourself better and influence others.

[3] Ray Dalio, *Principles* (Simon & Schuster, 2017).

Chapter Seven

HOW TO FIND YOUR PERSONALITY TYPE

All of these personality models, including the Personality Map, are only useful if they reflect reality. Many of them, like Big Five and DISC, have significant research backing them up to prove their validity, while others are more rooted in observation. We can discuss the scientific basis for personality traits and the trade-offs of each personality model forever, but sometimes the best way to understand an abstract concept like personality types is by seeing some examples.

Personality types are not popular because of their research papers—they are popular because they line up with how most people experience the world in their daily life. We already know these types intuitively from our own observations; a personality model like DISC gives us labels for them.

Traditionally, the most reliable way to measure someone's personality traits and detect their natural personality type was through questionnaire-style assessments. These assessments could range from a few dozen questions to hundreds.

Table 7.1 Methods of determining personality type.

METHOD	BENEFITS	FLAWS
Questionnaires	• High accuracy. • Widespread familiarity and acceptance.	• Time-consuming. • Susceptible to manipulation and bias from the person. • Requires participation from the person.
Text sample analysis	• Reliable accuracy. • Fast and convenient for individual analysis. • Does not require participation from the person.	• Requires sufficient text samples from people. • Susceptible to inaccuracy from people who intentionally modify their writing style.
Attribute analysis	• Only scalable method for analyzing large groups. • Makes predictions possible with limited data. • Does not require participation from people.	• Only moderate accuracy, especially with small number of attributes. • Requires structured dataset.

Recently, artificial intelligence has enabled two new methods to measure someone's personality: text sample analysis and attribute analysis. Text sample analysis functions just like it sounds: it analyzes the content and style within a block of text to determine the most likely personality type of the author. Attribute analysis uses more structured data, like someone's job titles, employers, skills, and interests to calculate the most likely personality type. Both of these methods allow us to detect a person's personality type without requiring them to complete a questionnaire. This is a remarkable advancement that opens the door to understanding anyone's personality, even for new use cases like sales, recruiting, marketing, and more.

Each of the three methods has its own benefits and flaws (see Table 7.1), and we will get into the details of how each one works later. For now, you just need to know what these options are, and why you might choose to use one of them.

The goal of Personality AI is to provide the most accurate possible personality profile for someone, based on the data and resources you have available. By combining these three methods of personality detection, you have a tool for almost any situation.

Chapter Eight

TAKE A PERSONALITY ASSESSMENT

In order to understand the intricacies of other people's personalities, it's first necessary to understand your own. In chapter 9, we'll cover the details of each personality archetype such as strengths, blind spots, motivations and work style. To identify your own personality type based on DISC, use the link to our website below to take a free personality assessment. The assessment should take you about 15 minutes to complete. Once you've finished it, read on to learn all about your personality type.

To take the free personality assessment, visit www.crystalknows.com/personality.

USING YOUR PERSONALITY AT WORK ——————

Finding your home on the Personality Map can be a fun, rewarding experience that helps you understand yourself on a deeper level. However, when you learn how to apply it in real life, you will find that it can be an extremely powerful tool for unlocking productivity and skills that you didn't know you had.

At work, we need to make decisions every day about how we spend our time, who we interact with, and what goals we pursue. When you understand your personality accurately, and have a common language to describe it, you can support each of these decisions with real data.

With this information, you are navigating your career with a map, rather than your gut feelings. In the next chapter, you will be able to learn the detailed implications of your personality type, along with the jobs that are likely to put you into a position to thrive.

Chapter Nine

THE 16 PERSONALITY TYPES

By now, you should know the personality type that best fits with your typical behavior patterns. In this chapter, we will describe each of the 16 types in more detail, with information like communication style, work preferences, strengths, blind spots, and more.

<u>You can feel free to skip ahead to your type.</u> Make sure to check back and read through the others, especially if you learn that one of your close connections, friends, or family members has a particular type (this is the one thing you should do if you want to see an immediate life impact from reading this book).

TYPE D: THE CAPTAIN

People with the *D (Captain)* personality type tend to be assertive, intense, and ambitious. They are usually pragmatic, results-oriented executors who work quickly and make decisions with firmness and objectivity.

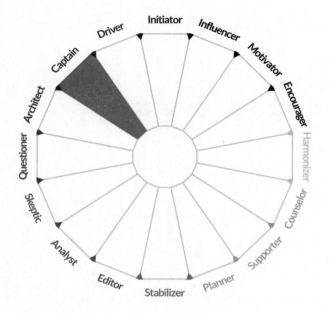

Figure 9.1 Type D: The Captain.

With a position on the top left of the Personality Map (see Figure 9.1), Captains prefer more independence and may be drained when others expect them to be more collaborative. They also may prefer to be in control over a situation, rather than in a position to react to others.

Personality Traits

Captains tend to ...

- Be resourceful, strong-willed, and self-reliant in pursuing goals.

- Enjoy engaging others in competitive situations.

- Place high expectations on performance from themselves and others.

- Enjoy lively debate.

- Resist influence from others.

Strengths and Blind Spots

Every personality archetype has strengths and blind spots, and these are often amplified in professional settings where we encounter a diverse group of people with vastly different backgrounds and value systems.

Strengths that are typically associated with the D personality type include ...

- Communicating directly, using facts and informal language.

- Focusing on results and realistic expectations.

- Being very firm and conclusive when making decisions.

- Using a goal-oriented approach to assigning work, omitting unnecessary details.

- Operating with a sense of urgency.

- Motivating others by creating competitive challenges.

- Directing others in an impersonal manner with clarity and precision.

- Expressing a desire for control and autonomy.

Blind spots that are typically associated with the D personality type include ...

- Failing to involve others in problem-solving due to desire for an immediate solution.

- Omitting too many details for the sake of brevity.

- Displaying impatience when providing detailed instruction.

- Having the urge to criticize others who do not share a sense of urgency.

- Maintaining control by delegating responsibility but not authority.

- Directing others so forcefully that they don't ask questions or discuss potential problems.

- Reacting aggressively when others try to limit authority or autonomy.

- Working with such a sense of urgency that it may cause others unnecessary stress.

Communication Preferences

Conversations	Conversation should be direct and straightforward, using a confident and assertive tone.
Meetings	Meetings should be very brief, to the point, and only scheduled when necessary.
Emails	Emails should be brief, business-like, and concise.
Feedback	Feedback should be direct, actionable, and focused on the most important facts.
Conflict	Conflict should be addressed objectively and in a timely manner.

Motivators and Stressors

When people experience pain, stress, or dissatisfaction at work, it can usually be attributed to energy-draining activities. Therefore, it's important to know what kinds of activities energize each personality type and what activities drain them.

Captains tend to be motivated and energized by ...

- Completing ambitious projects on a tight deadline.

- Taking primary responsibility and ownership over large projects.

- Making decisions quickly with limited data.

- Making decisions on behalf of other people.

- Setting up and participating in competitions.

- Seeing tangible, measurable results, milestones, and accomplishments.

- Providing goal-focused direction to others without needing to provide detailed instructions.

Captains tend to be stressed and drained by ...

- Paying close attention to the needs and concerns of other people.

- Playing an exclusive supporting role on a team.

- Responding to difficult situations with empathy and compassion.

- Promoting teamwork and cooperation between multiple parties.

- Following up and checking in with other people when they are dealing with a challenge.

- Taking lots of time to understand how people are feeling about a change.

- Building long-term trust and loyalty with consistent, predictable behavior.

Best Jobs for a Captain

Captains tend to gravitate toward positions of authority. They can be huge sources of motivation, and they set an aggressive pace meant to achieve results as efficiently as possible. They can also be relentlessly competitive, with themselves and with others. Asking a Captain to do anything they perceive as tedious or mundane will likely result in them either ignoring the request or delegating it to someone else.

Common jobs for Captains include:

- CEO

- Executive

- Founder

- Entrepreneur

- Lawyer

- Operations manager

- Police officer

- Director

TYPE Di: THE DRIVER

People with the *Di (Driver)* personality type are typically assertive, capable of putting themselves forward boldly, and resistant to influence from others. They may be seen as decisive, forceful, and persuasive when convincing others to work toward their goals.

With a position on the upper top left of the Personality Map (see Figure 9.2), Drivers are likely to take charge of things, setting the pace for others. They are usually skilled negotiators and persuasive when they want to convince others to adopt their viewpoint.

Personality Traits

Drivers tend to ...

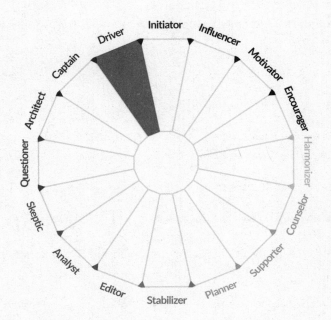

Figure 9.2 Type Di: The Driver.

- Be eager to take charge of things.

- Resist influence from others.

- Be vocal about opinions and ideas.

- Pursue large, ambitious goals with speed and bursts of intensity.

- Compete and debate with others.

Strengths and Blind Spots

Every personality archetype has strengths and blind spots, and these are often amplified in professional settings where we encounter a diverse group of people with vastly different backgrounds and value systems.

Strengths that are typically associated with the Di personality type include ...

- Being quick, independent, and firm when making decisions.

- Taking action with limited information.

- Seeking responsibility, autonomy, and decision-making ownership over results.

- Using verbal inspiration to direct others.

- Effectively delegating responsibility for detailed tasks.

Blind spots that are typically associated with the Di personality type include ...

- Working with a sense of urgency that may cause others unnecessary stress.

- Overdelegating responsibility to follow through on details.

- Trying to maintain too much control over results.

- Providing insufficient structure for people who need a defined approach to work.

- Reacting aggressively when others try to limit authority or autonomy.

- Pursuing too many new ideas or opportunities at once.

Communication Preferences

Conversations	Be confident, assertive, and straightforward in conversation, keeping in mind that they may only retain the most important parts.
Meetings	Meetings should be spontaneous, to the point, and not last a very long time.
Emails	Emails should be short, to the point, and contain very little detail.
Feedback	Feedback should be direct, actionable, and focused on the most important points.
Conflict	Conflict should be addressed openly and with a problem-solving mindset.

Motivators and Stressors

When people experience pain, stress, or dissatisfaction at work, it can usually be attributed to energy-draining activities. Therefore, it's important to know what kinds of activities energize each personality type and what activities drain them.

Drivers tend to be motivated and energized by ...

- Presenting ideas and strategies to groups of people.

- Directing and motivating others to improve their performance.

- Looking for new opportunities without much guidance.

- Communicating with quick conversations and messages, only when necessary.

- Setting up and participating in competitions.

- Making decisions on behalf of other people.

- Completing ambitious projects on a tight deadline.

- Taking primary responsibility and ownership over large projects.

Drivers tend to be stressed and drained by ...

- Staying consistent and predictable within a structured environment.

- Promoting teamwork and cooperation between others.

- Providing detailed analyses and reports.

- Analyzing all aspects of an important decision.

- Taking time to understand how people are feeling about a recent change.

Best Jobs for a Driver

Drivers are constantly seeking new opportunities for advancement, and they typically thrive in environments where they can produce immediate results and make tangible progress. They will likely do well with competition and are most satisfied with a high degree of control and authority over their work.

Common jobs for people with the Driver personality type are:

- Sales representative

- Account executive

- Recruiter

- Director of talent acquisition

- Founder

- Entrepreneur

- Chief executive officer

- Business executive

- Sales director

- Product manager

TYPE DI: THE INITIATOR

People with the *DI (Initiator)* personality type tend to approach people and situations in an energetic, lively manner. They are likely to enjoy the challenge of meeting new people and winning them over with strong social skills and a knack for being persuasive.

With a position on the middle top of the Personality Map (see Figure 9.3), Initiators are typically perceived as more extraverted, and

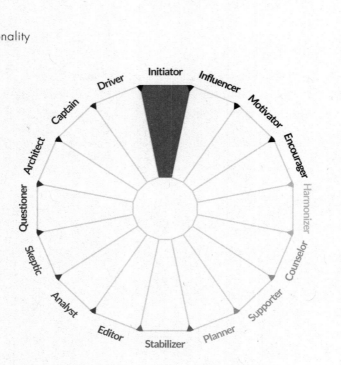

Figure 9.3 Type DI: The Initiator.

others may find themselves very engaged and absorbed in interactions. Initiators tend to communicate clearly and vividly to others using an emotionally expressive and demonstrative style.

Personality Traits

Initiators tend to ...

- Approach people and situations in an energetic, lively manner.

- Eagerly take charge of social situations.

- Be vocal about opinions and ideas.

- Work with intensity and a sense of adventure.

- Use charisma to bring people together, build rapport, and share ideas.

Strengths and Blind Spots

Every personality archetype has strengths and blind spots, and these are often amplified in professional settings where we encounter a diverse group of people with vastly different backgrounds and value systems.

Strengths that are typically associated with the DI personality type include ...

- Taking ownership and responsibility over results.

- Using verbal inspiration to direct others.

- Presenting the big picture enthusiastically.

- Quickly spotting new opportunities for advancement.

- Taking necessary risks and making bold decisions.

- Making decisions without all of the information.

- Creating novel solutions to challenging problems.

Blind spots that are typically associated with the DI personality type include ...

- Delegating too much and losing sight of the details.

- Being too controlling over results.

- Providing limited structure for people who appreciate a defined work environment.

- Jumping between too many new ideas or opportunities simultaneously.

- Working at a pace so fast that it may cause others stress.

- Having trouble following consistent, predictable routines.

- Being sarcastic too often, which may cause miscommunication with more literal people.

Communication Preferences

Conversations	Make sure you stay objective and avoid getting easily captivated or swayed by their persuasion skills.
Meetings	Meetings should be short and spontaneous, without a rigid agenda.
Emails	Emails should be concise and only include the most important information.
Feedback	Feedback should be specific and focused on the most critical points.
Conflict	Conflict should be used to improve and discover better solutions; focus on addressing an issue directly and presenting a way to fix it.

Motivators and Stressors

When people experience pain, stress, or dissatisfaction at work, it can usually be attributed to energy-draining activities. Therefore, it's important to know what kinds of activities energize each personality type and what activities drain them.

Initiators tend to be motivated and energized by ...

- Assigning detailed and analytical work to other people.

- Directing and motivating others to improve their performance.

- Creating new relationships and winning people over.

- Presenting new ideas to an audience.

- Seeking new opportunities with minimal direction.

- Taking calculated risks when presented with an opportunity.

- Making decisions quickly with limited data.

- Bouncing and riffing between multiple ideas at once.

- Taking ownership over big initiatives.

Initiators tend to be stressed and drained by ...

- Structured and consistent daily agendas.

- Providing one-on-one coaching and step-by-step instructions.

- Facilitating teamwork between others.

- Researching previous ways people have accomplished goals to improve performance.

- Minimizing risk with redundancy and analysis.

- Helping other people make plans.

- Clarifying information for others in an organized way.

- Communicating the detailed aspects of an important decision.

Best Jobs for an Initiator

Initiators thrive in positions where they can pursue ambitious goals, advance quickly, and earn the recognition of their peers. They will typically be very comfortable with competitive environments and may be stressed by environments that are very rigid or structured in their culture.

Common jobs for people with the DI personality type are:

- Journalist

- Chief marketing officer

- Marketing manager

- Marketing director

- Sales representative

- Account executive

- Recruiter

- Director of talent acquisition

- Founder

- Entrepreneur

TYPE ID: THE INFLUENCER

People with the *Id (Influencer)* personality type tend to be energetic and adventurous, communicating with casual language, bold statements, and a focus on the big picture. They are likely to have an easy, relaxed, casual manner when speaking or interacting with others and enjoy the challenge of meeting new people.

With a position on the upper top right of the Personality Map (see Figure 9.4), Influencers are typically known for their social skills, creativity, and charisma. They can clearly and vividly appeal to others using an emotionally expressive and demonstrative style, often able to convince them to take action.

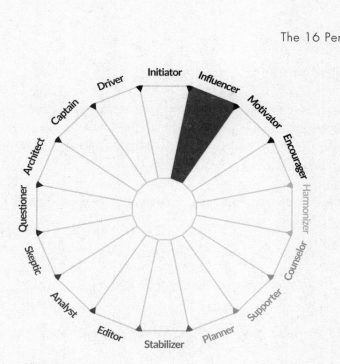

Figure 9.4 Type ID: The Influencer.

Personality Traits

Influencers tend to …

- Enjoy the challenge of meeting new people.

- Approach people and situations in an energetic, lively manner.

- Engage others with stories.

- Use charisma to bring people together, build rapport, and share ideas.

- Discuss high-level ideas and future possibilities.

Strengths and Blind Spots

Every personality archetype has strengths and blind spots, and these are often amplified in professional settings where we encounter a diverse group of people with vastly different backgrounds and value systems.

Strengths that are typically associated with the Id personality type include ...

- Trusting intuition and ability to improvise.

- Using positive, enthusiastic language when motivating others.

- Quickly spotting new opportunities for advancement.

- Solving problems by involving others in brainstorming and open discussion.

- Delegating responsibility for detailed tasks.

- Bringing energy and a sense of adventure to a team.

- Placing a high priority on personal interactions and relationships.

- Creating novel solutions to challenging problems.

Blind spots that are typically associated with the Id personality type include ...

- Struggling to follow predictable routines.

- Failing to evaluate problems realistically due to overly optimistic expectations.

- Pursuing too many new ideas at once.

- Trying to control all of the results.

- Stepping too far out of the details of important projects.

- Creating an environment that is too flexible for people who need a structured approach to work.

- Having the inability to limit time spent interacting with people.

Communication Preferences

Conversations	Use a casual, but assertive tone and describe things with enthusiasm and colorful language.
Meetings	Meetings should be in person when possible, without a specific agenda.
Emails	Emails should be casual, brief, and include high-level information.
Feedback	Feedback should be focused on the big picture and delivered with encouragement.
Conflict	Conflict should be productive and worthwhile; focus on talking through problems in order to find a creative solution.

Motivators and Stressors

When people experience pain, stress, or dissatisfaction at work, it can usually be attributed to energy-draining activities. Therefore, it's important to know what kinds of activities energize each personality type and what activities drain them.

Influencers tend to be motivated and energized by ...

- Finding new opportunities without much guidance.
- Regularly interacting with a large, diverse group of people.
- Fostering new relationships and convincing others.
- Exploring multiple ideas at once.
- Assigning analytical tasks to other people.
- Thinking on their feet and figuring things out as they go.
- Participating in group discussions and brainstorming sessions.
- Taking the time to understand how someone else thinks.
- Providing verbal encouragement and telling stories.

Influencers tend to be stressed and drained by ...

- Considering all aspects of a key decision.
- Following procedures and routines.
- Taking time to think through a problem before making a final decision.
- Inspecting and maintaining high-quality results.
- Spending a lot of time to research the root causes of a problem.
- Frequently asking factual, clarifying questions.
- Providing clear, step-by-step instructions.
- Communicating primarily in writing.
- Minimizing risk with structure, redundancy, and analysis.

Best Jobs for an Influencer

Influencers thrive in environments where they can explore new things, engage with others, and learn through open discussion and brainstorming. They are well-suited to lead group conversations and describe a vision for other people to follow, and they are likely to feel stressed by an environment that has lots of rules and structure.

Common jobs for people with the Id personality type are:

- Chief marketing officer

- Marketing manager

- Marketing director

- Sales representative

- Recruiter

- Director of talent acquisition

- Founder

- Entrepreneur

- Public relations director

- Public relations manager

TYPE I: THE MOTIVATOR

People with the *I (Motivator)* personality type tend to be enthusiastic, cheerful, and outgoing. They typically have an easy, relaxed, and casual manner when speaking or interacting with others.

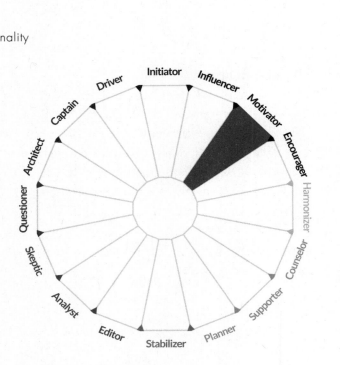

Figure 9.5 Type I: The Motivator.

With a position on the top right of the Personality Map (see Figure 9.5), Motivators are usually open and easy to approach, and are likely to be frequently involved with other people. Most Motivators enjoy being with others so much that they often find ways to include interactions with others as part of their daily activities.

Personality Traits

Motivators tend to …

- Appreciate interacting with others.

- Notice others quickly and help them feel comfortable in new groups.

- Easily build rapport, even after meeting someone new.

- Entertain others at a party.

- Enjoy the challenge of meeting new people.

Strengths and Blind Spots

Every personality archetype has strengths and blind spots, and these are often amplified in professional settings where we encounter a diverse group of people with vastly different backgrounds and value systems.

Strengths that are typically associated with the I personality type include ...

- Prioritizing relationships and personal interactions.

- Facilitating group brainstorming to find solutions to problems.

- Offering lots of verbal encouragement when developing others.

- Communicating in a spontaneous, emotionally expressive manner.

- Quickly improvising based on intuition.

- Using flexible schedules and open-ended approaches to time management.

- Understanding how to motivate other people to take action.

- Bringing energy and a sense of fun to a team.

Blind spots that are typically associated with the I personality type include ...

- Being overly optimistic about people or situations.

- Spending more time interacting with people than completing tasks.

- Having trouble following consistent, predictable routines.

- Having difficulty limiting time spent with people.

- Trusting gut feelings when more planning is necessary.

- Providing insufficient structure for people who need a defined approach to work.

- Getting distracted by multiple new ideas and failing to focus.

- Avoiding decisions that potentially involve losing approval or looking bad.

Communication Preferences

Conversations	Project a casual tone, use humor and personal anecdotes frequently, and describe past events with colorful language.
Meetings	Meetings should be done in person when possible, without a rigid agenda.
Emails	Emails should be friendly, casual, and personal.
Feedback	Feedback should be focused on the high level and delivered with encouragement.
Conflict	Conflict should be addressed in a balanced, intentional way to avoid unnecessary or unproductive arguing.

Motivators and Stressors

When people experience pain, stress, or dissatisfaction at work, it can usually be attributed to energy-draining activities. Therefore, it's important to know what kinds of activities energize each personality type and what activities drain them.

Motivators tend to be motivated and energized by ...

- Frequently interacting with a diverse group of people.

- Participating in group discussions and brainstorming sessions.

- Encouraging others and sharing stories.

- Going on new adventures and pursuing abstract opportunities.

- Considering how someone else thinks.

- Bouncing between multiple ideas at once.

- Leaving their schedule open and flexible for spontaneous meetings throughout the day.

- Figuring things out as they go by thinking on their feet.

- Explaining things with emotional, expressive language.

Motivators tend to be stressed and drained by ...

- Solving problems with thorough analysis of the existing data.

- Spending a lot of time researching the root causes of a problem.

- Creating procedures, rules, and guidelines for other people to follow.

- Helping others become more methodical and efficient in their processes.

- Clarifying facts by asking specific questions.

- Taking time to think through a problem before making a final decision.

- Using writing as the primary means of communication.

- Working on projects independently and bringing results back to a group.

- Inspecting and maintaining high-quality results.

Best Jobs for a Motivator

Motivators thrive in positions where they can explore new ideas, discover new approaches to doing things, be creative, and consistently connect with people. They will likely prefer work environments that are more collaborative, where they can use their verbal skills to communicate a vision and persuade others.

Common jobs for people with the I personality type are:

- Public relations director

- Public relations manager

- Creative director

- Designer

- Realtor

- Travel agent

- Artist

- Musician

- Copywriter

TYPE Is: THE ENCOURAGER

People with the *Is (Encourager)* personality type tend to be warm, cheerful, and light-hearted. Since they tend to be positive and joyful, Encouragers are likely to find a great deal to appreciate in others.

With a position on the far top right of the Personality Map (see Figure 9.6), Encouragers have usually discovered that acceptance and approval from others can be won by means of their friendly behavior. Thus, they may feel most comfortable when engaging others in this way.

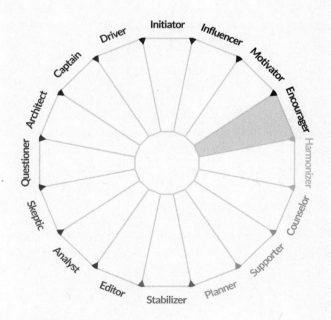

Figure 9.6 Type Is: The Encourager.

Personality Traits

Encouragers tend to ...

- Give others a sense of belonging and acceptance.

- Enjoy interacting with others.

- Have an outgoing and light-hearted approach, taking life as it comes.

- Avoid criticism and confrontation.

- Help others quickly feel comfortable in new groups.

Strengths and Blind Spots

Every personality archetype has strengths and blind spots, and these are often amplified in professional settings where we encounter a diverse group of people with vastly different backgrounds and value systems.

Strengths that are typically associated with the Is personality type include ...

- Developing others by offering plenty of verbal encouragement.

- Placing a high priority on personal interactions and relationships.

- Motivating other people to take action, even if they are nervous.

- Optimistically evaluating the capabilities of others.

- Bringing positive energy and warmth to a team.

- Communicating frequently and regularly.

- Using casual, friendly language with colleagues.

- Seeking the experience and ideas of others when solving problems.

Blind spots that are typically associated with the Is personality type include …

- Relying too much on gut feelings when detailed planning is necessary.

- Losing objectivity by becoming friendly and involved with others.

- Failing to evaluate problems realistically due to optimistic expectations of people or situations.

- Being overly focused on not losing approval or looking bad.

- Avoiding important tasks because they are spending too much time with people.

- Placating or appeasing people who are resisting or arguing.

- Having trouble with consistent, steady routines that may not be stimulating enough.

- Using a personal, emotional approach to problems that may get in the way of rational decision-making.

Communication Preferences

Conversations	Use a friendly, agreeable tone with colorful language, expressive gestures, and personal anecdotes.
Meetings	Meetings should be done in person when possible, without a specific agenda.
Emails	Emails should be approachable, friendly, and not too serious.
Feedback	Feedback should be thoroughly explained and delivered in a positive manner.
Conflict	Conflict should be focused on finding new solutions and approached with caution to avoid harming relationships.

Motivators and Stressors

When people experience pain, stress, or dissatisfaction at work, it can usually be attributed to energy-draining activities. Therefore, it's important to know what kinds of activities energize each personality type and what activities drain them.

Encouragers tend to be motivated and energized by ...

- Collaborating regularly alongside other people instead of working in isolation.

- Going on new adventures and pursuing abstract opportunities.

- Understanding and explaining the human impact of a big organizational decision.

- Using expressive, emotional anecdotes to make a story interesting.

- Providing verbal encouragement and telling stories.

- Teaching, coaching, and advising other people.

- Discussing matters as a group and brainstorming with others.

- Jumping between many ideas simultaneously.

Encouragers tend to be stressed and drained by ...

- Setting guidelines and clear rules for others.

- Developing more efficient processes.

- Taking primary ownership over timelines.

- Spending a lot of time to research the root causes of a problem.

- When directing others, focusing on what needs to be done, by whom and by when.

- Solving problems with thorough analysis of the existing data.

- Doing independent work and reporting on the results.

- Navigating large, complex systems.

Best Jobs for an Encourager

Encouragers typically seek environments that are conducive to group cooperation, harmony, and positivity. They can thrive in roles where they need to create and foster new relationships, and they can bring a lot to the table when brainstorming new ideas.

Common jobs for people with the Is personality type are:

- Public relations director

- Public relations manager

- Management consultant

- Executive coach

- Trainer

- Teacher

- Professor

- Financial advisor

- Minister

- Client services director

- Client services manager

- Director of partnerships

TYPE IS: THE HARMONIZER

People with the *IS (Harmonizer)* personality type tend to be warm, even-tempered, and accepting. Since they tend to be positive and joyful, Harmonizers are likely to seek lots of social interaction and affirmation.

With a position on the far right of the Personality Map (see Figure 9.7), Harmonizers are likely to approach the world with an open, trusting, and inviting attitude but also may shy away from interpersonal conflict in tough situations. It is likely very easy for them

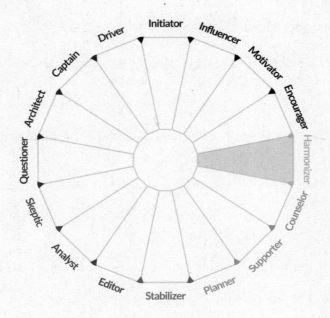

Figure 9.7 Type IS: The Harmonizer.

to give others the feeling of being understood and accepted for who they are, and to be accommodating rather than assertive.

Personality Traits

Harmonizers tend to ...

- Adapt to situations as they are.

- Foster an environment that gives others a sense of belonging.

- Get pleasure from spending time with others.

- Adjust easily to a wide range of styles.

- Avoid initiating conflict with others.

Strengths and Blind Spots

Every personality archetype has strengths and blind spots, and these are often amplified in professional settings where we encounter a diverse group of people with vastly different backgrounds and value systems.

Strengths that are typically associated with the IS personality type include ...

- Measuring the capabilities of others in an optimistic way.

- Communicating in an informal manner, mixing personal talk with business discussions.

- Frequently communicating to keep others informed.

- Approaching problem-solving from a personal or emotional angle.

- Being friendly and welcoming with coworkers.

- Involving people in discussions of how things will be done.

- Considering the impact on other people when making decisions.

- Getting guidance from others when trying to overcome challenges.

Blind spots that are typically associated with the IS personality type include ...

- Too easily giving in to people who are argumentative.

- Putting off decisions that may negatively impact someone.

- Becoming too close with others and then being unable to judge them objectively.

- Being unrealistically optimistic when considering big problems.

- Avoiding decisions that potentially involve losing approval or looking bad.

- Displaying discomfort when communicating with hostile or aggressive people.

- Minimizing negative feedback, leaving others unclear about a problem.

- Correcting or redoing work rather than confronting someone who becomes hostile.

Communication Preferences

Conversations	Use lots of emotional expression and try to be very perceptive of how they are feeling in the moment, even if what they are saying is mostly positive.
Meetings	Meetings should be in-person in a relaxed setting.
Emails	Emails should be friendly, casual, and personal.
Feedback	Feedback should be thoroughly explained and delivered with encouragement.
Conflict	Conflict should be approached with patience and thoughtfulness to avoid harming relationships.

Motivators and Stressors

When people experience pain, stress, or dissatisfaction at work, it can usually be attributed to energy-draining activities. Therefore, it's important to know what kinds of activities energize each personality type and what activities drain them.

Harmonizers tend to be motivated and energized by ...

- Collaborating with other people rather than working alone.

- Mentoring and advising others on tough situations.

- Making themselves available for the personal and emotional needs of other people.

- Using diplomacy and natural openness to solve problems.

- Participating in group discussions and brainstorming sessions.

- Articulating the human impact of an organizational decision.

- Asking questions from more experienced colleagues to learn how to do something.

Harmonizers tend to be stressed and drained by ...

- Directing others to follow rules and procedures.

- Interacting with a reserved, business-like approach.

- Monitoring and measuring results closely.

- Finding ways to make processes more efficient.

- Providing critical feedback to others about how they can improve their performance.

- Correcting people and showing them how to do things the right way.

- Monitoring a timeline and ensuring a project follows a rigid process.

- Navigating large, complex systems.

Best Jobs for a Harmonizer

Harmonizers thrive in positions where they can interact with lots of other people throughout the day and facilitate things. They are likely to be most comfortable working in peaceful, welcoming environments that are less competitive and more collaborative.

Common jobs for people with the IS personality type are:

- Guidance counselor

- Mediator

- Trainer

- Teacher

- Career advisor

- Financial advisor

- Community organizer

- Client services director

- Customer support representative

- Director of partnerships

TYPE SI: THE COUNSELOR

People with the *Si (Counselor)* personality type tend to be even-tempered and accepting. Empathetic and supportive, they may seek to help others frequently and sincerely.

With a position on the bottom right of the Personality Map (see Figure 9.8), Counselors are likely to show caring and understanding when listening to others. Their considerate and accepting responses create a warm atmosphere that encourages others to express their feelings without any fear of embarrassment or rejection.

Personality Traits

Counselors tend to ...

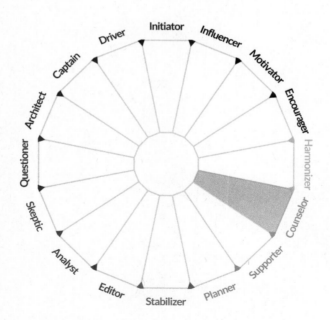

Figure 9.8 Type Si: The Counselor.

- Express caring and understanding toward other people.

- Help and support other people in their goals.

- Adapt to difficult situations.

- Reduce conflict with others.

- Easily adjust to someone else's style.

Strengths and Blind Spots

Every personality archetype has strengths and blind spots, and these are often amplified in professional settings where we encounter a diverse group of people with vastly different backgrounds and value systems.

Strengths that are typically associated with the Si personality type include ...

- Promoting the benefits of teamwork and cooperation when motivating others.

- Providing a calming, stabilizing presence for others in tough situations.

- Building trusting relationships by providing predictability and rewarding loyalty.

- Including others in sharing their experience when solving problems.

- Resolving conflict between others with diplomacy and sensitivity.

Blind spots that are typically associated with the Si personality type include . . .

- Not being forceful or assertive when necessary.

- Becoming uncomfortable when handling aggressive people.

- Having trouble detaching and being productive in emotionally charged situations.

- Displaying discomfort when managing people who actively resist close supervision.

- Reacting emotionally instead of objectively to critical feedback.

Communication Preferences

Conversations	Use a friendly, agreeable, warm tone and try to relate to them personally, without getting into business discussion too quickly.
Meetings	Meetings should be done in person when possible, with a prepared agenda.
Emails	Emails should be warm, sincere, and expressive.
Feedback	Feedback should be thoughtfully explained and delivered with empathy.
Conflict	Conflict should be handled diplomatically, allowing all sides to voice their opinions and hear the others.

Motivators and Stressors

When people experience pain, stress, or dissatisfaction at work, it can usually be attributed to energy-draining activities. Therefore, it's important to know what kinds of activities energize each personality type and what activities drain them.

Counselors tend to be motivated and energized by ...

- Building long-term trust and loyalty with consistent, predictable behavior.

- Asking other people how they feel about an upcoming change.

- Advising people as they deal with a challenge.

- Paying attention to the needs and concerns of other people.

- Solving problems with diplomacy and openness.

Counselors tend to be stressed and drained by ...

- Communication that is too blunt or direct.

- Considering many factors to make decisions.

- Making decisions quickly with limited data.

- Using a forceful approach to direct and develop others.

- Critically questioning existing practices and procedures.

- Taking primary ownership over processes and timelines.

Best Jobs for a Counselor

Counselors generally enjoy peaceful, welcoming environments where they can take time to collaborate and learn more about other people. They thrive with cooperation and harmony and fit well in jobs where they can frequently give and receive verbal affirmation.

Common jobs for people with the Si personality type are:

- Teacher

- Professor

- Financial advisor

- Ministry

- Client services manager

- Director of partnerships

- Human resources manager

- Therapist

- Counselor

- Executive assistant

- Customer success and support

TYPE S: THE SUPPORTER

People with the S (Supporter) personality type tend to be calm, patient, and respectful in their interactions with others. Rarely angered or excited, they are likely to work to maintain a peaceful and harmonious environment.

With a position on the lower right of the Personality Map (see Figure 9.9), Supporters are likely to demonstrate their thoughtfulness and sincerity by listening patiently when responding to the needs and requests of others. Respectfully considering the thoughts and feelings of others, they are likely able to respond empathetically in difficult or stressful situations.

Personality Traits

Supporters tend to ...

- Listen patiently to the needs and requests of others.

- Work considerately and cooperatively with others.

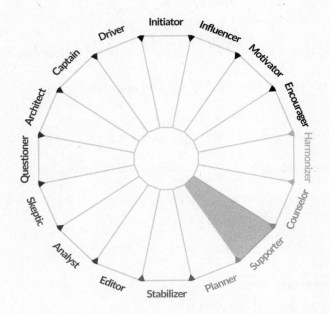

Figure 9.9 Type S: The Supporter.

- Be uncomfortable with aggressive or hostile people.

- Avoid overly competitive situations.

- Take direction from a trusted leader.

Strengths and Blind Spots

Every personality archetype has strengths and blind spots, and these are often amplified in professional settings where we encounter a diverse group of people with vastly different backgrounds and value systems.

Strengths that are typically associated with the S personality type include ...

- Following up by checking back on a regular basis and being available to help.

- Responding to questions with patience and understanding.

- Asking for feedback at regular intervals.

- Being attentive to the needs and concerns of other people.

Blind spots that are typically associated with the S personality type include ...

- Not being direct when communicating negative information.

- Being too passive when assertiveness is necessary.

- Avoiding confrontation and not giving feedback to others who may need it.

- Delaying decisions involving interpersonal conflict.

Communication Preferences

Conversations	Use a calm, agreeable, warm tone and be very considerate of their feelings, asking questions to understand where they may have concerns or thoughts.
Meetings	Meetings should have a prepared agenda and be done in person.
Emails	Emails should be warm, sincere, and expressive.
Feedback	Feedback should be thoughtfully explained and delivered with empathy.
Conflict	Conflict should be handled with caution, as it can escalate and result in hurt feelings.

Motivators and Stressors

When people experience pain, stress, or dissatisfaction at work, it can usually be attributed to energy-draining activities. Therefore, it's important to know what kinds of activities energize each personality type and what activities drain them.

Supporters tend to be motivated and energized by ...

- Asking for feedback regularly.

- Playing a supporting role on the team and staying out of the spotlight.

- Responding to difficult situations with empathy and compassion.

- Promoting teamwork and cooperation between parties.

- Listening to questions from other people and responding thoughtfully.

Supporters tend to be stressed and drained by ...

- Frequently working on a tight deadline.

- Making decisions on behalf of other people without much group input.

- Assigning tasks with major goals, rather than detailed instruction.

- Engaging in competition with others.

- Being in the spotlight or the center of attention.

Best Jobs for a Supporter

Supporters thrive in positions where they are able to attend to the needs of others, build long-term trust, and have lots of daily interaction. They appreciate predictable, calm, collaborative environments and may work most effectively when they can make plans for the future and stick to them most of the time.

Common jobs for people with the S personality type are:

- Human resources manager

- Human resources director

- Therapist

- Counselor

- Executive assistant

- Customer success

- Customer support

- Physician assistant

- Pediatrician

- Nurse

- Nurse practitioner

- Dental hygienist

TYPE Sc: THE PLANNER

People with the *Sc (Planner)* personality type tend to be easygoing and fairly even-keeled in their temperament. They often provide predictability and consistency in their interactions and seek the same thing in return.

Figure 9.10 Type Sc: The Planner.

With a position on the lower bottom right of the Personality Map (see Figure 9.10), Planners may be more detail-oriented than most people, and be very comfortable letting others direct conversations. They may hesitate to be assertive with their desires at times in order to maintain a peaceful environment and avoid interpersonal conflict.

Personality Traits

Planners tend to …

- Work cooperatively with others.

- Follow trusted leaders.

- Be humble, unassuming, and reluctant to talk about accomplishments.

- Accommodate the requests of others rather than risk conflict.

- Seek predictability and consistency.

Strengths and Blind Spots

Every personality archetype has strengths and blind spots, and these are often amplified in professional settings where we encounter a diverse group of people with vastly different backgrounds and value systems.

Strengths that are typically associated with the Sc personality type include ...

- Approaching decision-making carefully.

- Being highly organized and attentive to details.

- Using low-risk solutions that have proven effective in the past.

- Using a structured approach to developing others whenever possible.

Blind spots that are typically associated with the Sc personality type include ...

- Not bringing underlying conflict to the surface when necessary.

- Delaying making decisions perceived as high-risk.

- Hesitating to try solutions that have not been tested.

- Spending too much time analyzing information before making a decision.

Communication Preferences

Conversations	Discuss important issues in person, ask plenty of questions, and leave lots of time to fully understand what they are feeling.
Meetings	Meetings should be done in person when possible, with a specific agenda.
Emails	Emails should be warm, sincere, and well-formatted.
Feedback	Feedback should be thoroughly detailed and delivered with recommendations.
Conflict	Conflict should be handled with caution and tact, as Planners prefer to ease into difficult conversations rather than rush them.

Motivators and Stressors

When people experience pain, stress, or dissatisfaction at work, it can usually be attributed to energy-draining activities. Therefore, it's important to know what kinds of activities energize each personality type and what activities drain them.

Planners tend to be motivated and energized by ...

- Receiving consistent feedback.

- Establishing daily routines.

- Organizing and clarifying information for other people.

- Presenting and analyzing all aspects of an important decision.

Planners tend to be stressed and drained by ...

- Presenting ideas and strategies to groups of people.

- Directing and pushing others to improve their performance.

- Looking for new opportunities without any guidance.

- Bouncing between multiple ideas at once.

- Thinking on their feet and figuring things out as they go.

Best Jobs for a Planner

Planners can be most effective detecting risks and potential consequences of a decision, creating schedules for others, and providing supporting information. They are usually adept at managing change in a smooth, diplomatic way, making sure everyone is on the same page.

Common jobs for people with the Sc personality type are:

- Research director

- Researcher

- Pharmacist

- Quality assurance analyst

- Accountant

- Scientist

- Service technician

- Risk management

- Physician assistant

TYPE SC: THE STABILIZER

People with the *SC (Stabilizer)* personality type tend to be even-tempered, fairly reserved, and cautious when making decisions. Stabilizers typically offer predictability and consistency in their interactions and are likely to desire the same from others.

With a position on the middle bottom of the Personality Map (see Figure 9.11), Stabilizers are usually quick to agree with others, accommodating their viewpoints rather than risking conflict. They can be extremely perceptive, detail-oriented, and meticulous in their work. Socially, they may easily adjust to a wide range of personal styles and maintain harmony in any situation.

Personality Traits

Stabilizers tend to ...

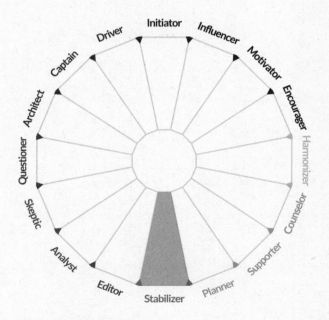

Figure 9.11 Type SC: The Stabilizer.

- Give support and guidance to others.

- Make others feel at ease.

- Appreciate consistency and predictability.

- Accommodate others rather than risk conflict.

- Collaborate peacefully with a group.

Strengths and Blind Spots

Every personality archetype has strengths and blind spots, and these are often amplified in professional settings where we encounter a diverse group of people with vastly different backgrounds and value systems.

Strengths that are typically associated with the SC personality type include ...

- Showing people how to do things in a step-by-step manner.

- Using a predictable routine and established schedules.

- Working with a specific plan for how things are going to be done.

- Giving specific, detailed information when assigning work.

Blind spots that are typically associated with the SC personality type include ...

- Putting off high-risk decisions for too long.

- Hesitating to try solutions that have not been tested but may be effective.

- Deferring high-impact decisions to higher levels of authority or requiring sign-off.

- Not being forceful or assertive when necessary.

Communication Preferences

Conversations	Use a calm, deliberate approach and make sure to ask lots of questions to get them to open up.
Meetings	Meetings should be formally scheduled and have a prepared agenda.
Emails	Emails should be sincere and well-formatted.
Feedback	Feedback should be thoroughly detailed and delivered with recommendations.
Conflict	Conflict should be used to solve important problems, but should also be handled with significant caution.

Motivators and Stressors

When people experience pain, stress, or dissatisfaction at work, it can usually be attributed to energy-draining activities. Therefore, it's important to know what kinds of activities energize each personality type and what activities drain them.

Stabilizers tend to be motivated and energized by ...

- Providing one-on-one coaching and step-by-step instructions.

- Communicating primarily in writing.

- Researching previous ways people have accomplished goals to improve performance.

- Minimizing risk with structure, redundancy, and analysis.

- Providing specific, detailed information and reports.

- Helping other people make plans.

Stabilizers tend to be stressed and drained by ...

- Delegating detailed and analytical work to other people.

- Taking large risks in unpredictable situations.

- Making decisions quickly with limited data.

- Receiving a large volume of frequent critical feedback.

- Taking primary responsibility and ownership over large projects.

Best Jobs for a Stabilizer

Stabilizers thrive in positions where they can interact with lots of other people throughout the day and facilitate things. They are likely the most comfortable in peaceful, welcoming environments that are less competitive and more collaborative.

Common jobs for people with the SC personality type are:

- Copy Editor

- Researcher

- Pharmacist

- Quality assurance engineer

- Paralegal

- Accountant

- Scientist

- Service technician

- Risk management

TYPE CS: THE EDITOR

People with the *Cs (Editor)* personality type tend to be more reserved and solitary. Editors typically limit their professional contact with others to interactions that are more structured rather than informal, so they may find themselves hesitant to join in on casual group conversations.

With a position on the lower bottom left of the Personality Map (see Figure 9.12), Editors prefer to be serious and rational. People with

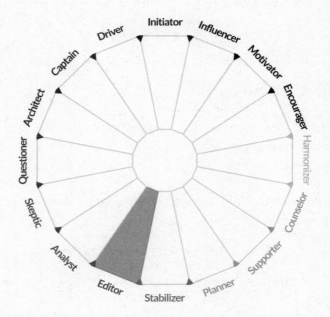

Figure 9.12 Type Cs: The Editor.

this archetype may enjoy logical arguments or interacting with people who use a more systematic or methodical approach. They also think carefully before speaking and typically use words precisely.

Personality Traits

Editors tend to …

- Take a private, independent approach to life.

- Be sensitive to other peoples' phoniness, insincerity, or arrogance.

- Appreciate guidance and direction from others.

- Separate emotions from decision-making.

- Be serious, exacting, and sometimes a perfectionist in their work.

Strengths and Blind Spots

Every personality archetype has strengths and blind spots, and these are often amplified in professional settings where we encounter a diverse group of people with vastly different backgrounds and value systems.

Strengths that are typically associated with the Cs personality type include …

- Using an analytical approach to solving problems.

- Considering many factors when making a decision.

- Gathering information and assessing risk before making decisions.

- Showing people how to do things in a step-by-step manner.

- Maintaining quality by asking questions frequently.

Blind spots that are typically associated with the Cs personality type include ...

- Spending more time working alone when collaboration would be more effective.

- Hesitating to try new solutions that have not been tested.

- Spending too much time analyzing information before making a decision.

- Overcomplicating solutions to simple problems.

- Deferring high-impact decisions to higher levels of authority or requiring sign-off.

- Expecting others to be as organized and attentive to detail as they are.

Communication Preferences

Conversations	Make sure you think carefully before speaking and use clear words that mean precisely what you want to convey, avoiding sarcasm.
Meetings	Meetings should be minimal, formally scheduled, and with a prepared agenda.
Emails	Emails should be clear, descriptive, and sincere.
Feedback	Feedback should be thoughtful, detailed, and delivered with logical reasoning.
Conflict	Conflict should be addressed in a rational way, in order to discover truth and bring underlying issues to the surface.

Motivators and Stressors

When people experience pain, stress, or dissatisfaction at work, it can usually be attributed to energy-draining activities. Therefore, it's important to know what kinds of activities energize each personality type and what activities drain them.

Editors tend to be motivated and energized by ...

- Carefully considering all aspects of an important decision.

- Taking time to think through a problem before making a final decision.

- Inspecting and maintaining high-quality results.

- Researching previous ways people have accomplished goals to improve performance.

- Frequently asking factual, clarifying questions.

Editors tend to be stressed and drained by ...

- Regularly interacting with a large group of people.

- Thinking on their feet and figuring things out as they go.

- Participating in group discussions and brainstorming sessions.

- Discussing abstract ideas instead of concrete ones.

- Providing verbal encouragement and telling stories.

Best Jobs for an Editor

Editors are most satisfied and productive when they are continuously building skills and expertise. They value stability and security, and are well-suited for process-oriented environments and roles that allow them to work with accuracy and precision.

Common jobs for people with the Cs personality type are:

- Medical technician

- Air traffic controller

- Quality assurance engineer

- Database administrator

- Accountant

- Scientist

- Data scientist

- Financial analyst

- Systems administrator

TYPE C: THE ANALYST

People with the C (Analyst) personality type tend to be objective, skeptical, and logical in their behavior. They are usually fiercely pragmatic and frequently solve problems with an analytical, fact-driven approach. They are likely to be more reserved in groups and may take a long time before they build enough trust to open up.

With a position on the bottom left of the Personality Map (see Figure 9.13), Analysts are likely to approach life in a serious manner. Preferring solitary activities, they are likely to guard their privacy and be more involved with their deep, independent thoughts than external stimuli.

Personality Traits

Analysts tend to ...

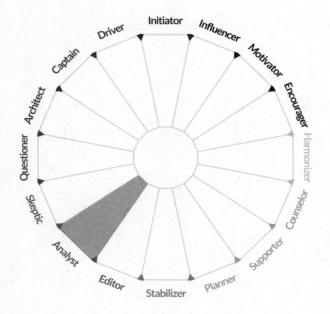

Figure 9.13 Type C: The Analyst.

- Prefer privacy and solitary activities.

- Make objective decisions, rather than emotional ones.

- Skeptically or realistically appraise people and situations.

- Be sensitive to lack of sincerity in others.

- Maintain a serious demeanor at work.

Strengths and Blind Spots

Every personality archetype has strengths and blind spots, and these are often amplified in professional settings where we encounter a diverse group of people with vastly different backgrounds and value systems.

Strengths that are typically associated with the C personality type include ...

- Taking time to think things through when making decisions.

- Providing clearly defined procedures when giving assignments.

- Using a deliberate, methodical approach when solving problems.

- Being comfortable analyzing large amounts of information.

- Giving work assignments in writing and requesting written feedback.

Blind spots that are typically associated with the C personality type include ...

- Seeking a perfect solution instead of a workable solution.

- Taking a lot of time gathering information and assessing risk before making decisions.

- Avoiding or resisting people who do not use a systematic approach to organizing work.

- Criticizing others who don't meet their standards for quality and accuracy.

- Checking in too frequently, with too many questions when someone needs more autonomy.

- Overcomplicating solutions to simple problems.

Communication Preferences

Conversations	Use a serious, business-like demeanor and ask strictly objective questions to fully understand what they are thinking.
Meetings	Meetings should be minimal, formally scheduled, and with a prepared agenda.
Emails	Emails should be clear, detailed, and factual.
Feedback	Feedback should be specific, detailed, and delivered with logical reasoning.
Conflict	Conflict should be viewed objectively to effectively bring underlying issues to the surface.

Motivators and Stressors

When people experience pain, stress, or dissatisfaction at work, it can usually be attributed to energy-draining activities. Therefore, it's important to know what kinds of activities energize each personality type and which activities drain them.

Analysts tend to be motivated and energized by ...

- Solving problems with thorough analysis of the existing data.

- Researching the root causes of a problem.

- Creating procedures, rules, and guidelines for other people to follow.

- Helping others become more methodical and efficient in their processes.

- Working on projects independently and bringing results back to a group.

Analysts tend to be stressed and drained by ...

- Brainstorming about far-out ideas instead of clear ones.

- Taking the time to understand how someone else thinks.

- Leaving their schedule open and flexible for spontaneous meetings throughout the day.

- Explaining things with emotional, expressive language.

Best Jobs for an Analyst

Analysts thrive in positions where they can take enough time to do their work with accuracy, precision, and the highest possible quality. They are likely to prefer independent work over lots of collaboration, and typically prefer more structured environments that have established rules and processes.

Common jobs for people with the C personality type are:

- Software engineer

- Mechanical engineer

- Chemical engineer

- Actuary

- Investment analyst

- Software developer

- Data scientist

- Financial analyst

- Systems administrator

- Director of engineering

TYPE Cd: THE SKEPTIC

People with the *Cd (Skeptic)* personality type tend to be more serious in their demeanor and very logical in their thinking. They tend to be most comfortable with thoughtful, independent work, and may relate to others in a more distant and detached manner.

With a position on the far left of the Personality Map (see Figure 9.14), Skeptics typically maintain autonomy and strong control over their

Figure 9.14 Type Cd: The Skeptic.

schedule. As their archetype suggests, they are very likely to be skeptical when people or companies make a bold claim without data to back it up. Skeptics place a high value on efficiency, accuracy, and logic.

Personality Traits

Skeptics tend to ...

- Seek personal space, privacy, and autonomy.

- Steer clear of large group activities.

- Relate to others in an independent and detached manner.

- Build trust or reveal personal information more slowly than most people.

- Make decisions without emotions clouding judgement.

Strengths and Blind Spots

Every personality archetype has strengths and blind spots, and these are often amplified in professional settings where we encounter a diverse group of people with vastly different backgrounds and value systems.

Strengths that are typically associated with the Cd personality type include ...

- Being straightforward, objective, and grounded in reality.

- Using an analytical approach to solving problems.

- Taking responsibility and ownership over results.

- Focusing on what needs to be done, by whom and by when.

- Developing others by specifying competency requirements and assessing performance.

Blind spots that are typically associated with the Cd personality type include ...

- Being critical of people who don't meet their standards for quality and accuracy.

- Overcomplicating solutions to simple problems.

- Being uncomfortable with small talk, saving time but missing out on its relational benefits.

- Spending time working alone when collaboration would be more effective.

- Reacting aggressively when others try to limit authority or autonomy.

Communication Preferences

Conversations	Use a direct, factual, and unemotional tone, providing literal and factual descriptions over colorful or embellished ones.
Meetings	Meetings should be minimal, formally scheduled, and with a prepared agenda.
Emails	Emails should be clear, detailed, and factual.
Feedback	Feedback should be specific, detailed, and delivered with logical reasoning.
Conflict	Conflict should be focused on addressing specific, underlying problems and finding practical solutions.

Motivators and Stressors

When people experience pain, stress, or dissatisfaction at work, it can usually be attributed to energy-draining activities. Therefore, it's important to know what kinds of activities energize each personality type and what activities drain them.

Skeptics tend to be motivated and energized by ...

- Creating specific policies and rules for others to follow.

- Developing more efficient processes.

- Having ownership over the quality of their work.

- When directing others, focusing on what needs to be done, by whom and by when.

- Navigating large, complex systems.

Skeptics tend to be stressed and drained by ...

- Collaborating regularly alongside other people at the expense of independence.

- Pursuing abstract opportunities.

- Understanding and explaining the human impact of a big organizational decision.

- Teaching, coaching, and advising other people.

- Displaying empathy when someone is dealing with an emotional situation.

Best Jobs for a Skeptic

Skeptics thrive in positions where they can work independently, find underlying problems, and make things more efficient. They are likely to be highly methodical in their work style and place a high value on accuracy and precision, so they tend to prefer environments that are more formal, structured, and give them opportunities to build their skills.

Common jobs for people with the Cd personality type are:

- Project manager

- Architect

- Sales operations manager

- Chief technology officer

- Investment analyst

- Software developer

- Software engineer

- Data scientist

- Financial analyst

- Systems administrator

- Director of engineering

TYPE CD: THE QUESTIONER

People with the CD (Questioner) personality type tend to remove emotions from decision-making as much as possible, valuing efficiency

Figure 9.15 Type CD: The Questioner.

and logic over intuition or social proof. They are usually more reserved in their interactions and may relate to others in a more distant and detached manner, building trust slowly.

With a position on the far left of the Personality Map (see Figure 9.15), Questioners typically prioritize personal space, privacy, and autonomy. Their matter-of-fact, unsentimental approach to people and situations allows them to maintain a comfortable distance, with less emotional involvement in decisions.

Personality Traits

Questioners tend to ...

- Speak with matter-of-fact, objective language.

- Act with purpose and focus.

- Pursue goals rather than spend much time interacting with others.

- Aggressively overcome opposition and competition.

- Be impatient when progress is blocked.

Strengths and Blind Spots

Every personality archetype has strengths and blind spots, and these are often amplified in professional settings where we encounter a diverse group of people with vastly different backgrounds and value systems.

Strengths that are typically associated with the CD personality type include ...

- Using a reserved, business-like approach when interacting with others.

- Developing efficient tactics that improve performance and maintain quality.

- Showing people how to do things in a logical sequence.

- Directing others in an unemotional manner with clarity and precision.

- Taking on complex, interconnected problems and making sense of them.

Blind spots that are typically associated with the CD personality type include ...

- Monitoring results closely to the point where they feel micromanaged.

- Appearing cold, detached, or uninvolved when interacting with others.

- Displaying frustration when standards for performance are not met.

- Criticizing people who don't meet their standards for quality and accuracy.

- Being overly brief or robotic in communication.

- Making changes quickly and decisively, potentially disrupting the work of others.

Communication Preferences

Conversations	Use a restrained, direct, unemotional demeanor and avoid making claims that you cannot back up.
Meetings	Meetings should be minimal, formally scheduled, and with a prepared agenda.
Emails	Emails should be clear, business-like, and factual.
Feedback	Feedback should be direct, critical, and delivered with logical reasoning.
Conflict	Conflict should be handled in a logical, unemotional, and well-informed way.

Motivators and Stressors

When people experience pain, stress, or dissatisfaction at work, it can usually be attributed to energy-draining activities. Therefore, it's important to know what kinds of activities energize each personality type and what activities drain them.

Questioners tend to be motivated and energized by ...

- Directing others to follow rules and procedures.

- Interacting with a reserved, business-like approach.

- Focusing on the primary reasons for a problem rather than the symptoms.

- Providing feedback to others about how they can improve their performance.

- Showing people how to do things the correct way.

- Completing projects on a strict timetable.

Questioners tend to be stressed and drained by ...

- Staying aware of the personal and emotional needs of other people.

- Checking in frequently to make sure people are on the same page.

- Opening up about emotional issues.

- Communicating in a friendly, casual tone.

- Asking questions from more experienced colleagues to learn how to do something.

Best Jobs for a Questioner

Questioners thrive in positions where they can be hyper-efficient, achieving results with minimal waste and distraction. This makes them well-suited for environments that are more autonomous and value accuracy, logic, and pragmatism.

Common jobs for people with the CD personality type are:

- Project manager

- Architect

- Sales operations manager

- Chief technology officer

- Finance director

- Chief financial officer

- Business strategist

- Compliance manager

- Compliance officer

TYPE DC: THE ARCHITECT

People with the *Dc (Architect)* personality type tend to be intense and use a more forceful approach to life than most people. Strong-willed and independent, they typically prefer pursuing their own path and directing their own activities rather than collaborating extensively with others.

With a position on the upper far left of the Personality Map (see Figure 9.16), Architects prefer to be serious and are more likely to spend energy on business-like, purposeful interactions with others rather than casual social ones. With a strong focus on results, they tend to desire control over those things that affect their ability to achieve goals and actively resist distractions along the way.

Personality Traits

Architects tend to ...

- Seek control over their environment.

- Focus more of their professional time on results than relationships.

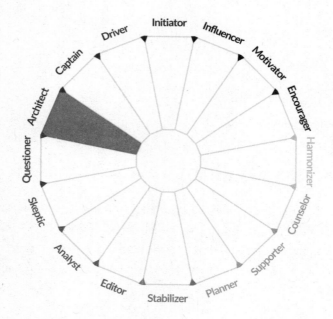

Figure 9.16 Type Dc: The Architect.

- Be diligent, strong-willed, and determined in their pursuit of goals.

- React to opposition with force, rather than passivity.

- Place high expectations on their own performance and that of others.

Strengths and Blind Spots

Every personality archetype has strengths and blind spots, and these are often amplified in professional settings where we encounter a diverse group of people with vastly different backgrounds and value systems.

Strengths that are typically associated with the Dc personality type include ...

- Being focused on results and realistic expectations.

- Maintaining efficiency and being oriented toward constant improvement in performance.

- Identifying specific ways to help others improve.

- Seeing the world through a clear, logical, factual lens.

- Carefully considering decisions perceived as high-risk.

- Communicating directly, using facts and precise language.

- Taking responsibility and ownership over results.

Blind spots that are typically associated with the Dc personality type include ...

- Being overly forceful and inflexible when providing instructions.

- Changing things too quickly without justifying the clear reasons for it.

- Using a very goal-oriented approach that might ignore important details.

- Addressing conflict with a firm, direct tone, which may be uncomfortable for some.

- Expressing critical feedback very quickly, without consideration for emotions.

Communication Preferences

Conversations	Be very direct, assertive, stay on topic, and orient toward business instead of small talk.
Meetings	Meetings should be brief and only scheduled when necessary.
Emails	Emails should be concisely written, business-like in tone, and factual in content.
Feedback	Feedback should be direct, critical, and focused on the results.
Conflict	Conflict should be addressed in a straightforward, logical way

Motivators and Stressors

When people experience pain, stress, or dissatisfaction at work, it can usually be attributed to energy-draining activities. Therefore, it's important to know what kinds of activities energize each personality type and which activities drain them.

Architects tend to be motivated and energized by ...

- Rapid feedback and clear communication.

- Considering many factors when making a decision.

- Monitoring results closely.

- Making decisions quickly with limited data.

- Using a forceful approach to direct and develop others.

- Critically questioning existing practices and procedures.

Architects tend to be stressed and drained by ...

- Frequent meetings in person or on the phone.

- Watching others take a lot of time to complete tasks.

- Delivering criticism in a gentle way.

- Making sure other people are feeling at peace with a big change before making it.

- Revealing emotions or underlying motivations.

- Collaborating and brainstorming in an open-ended format.

- Offering frequent verbal encouragement to others.

Best Jobs for an Architect

Architects are most satisfied and productive when they are learning as they go—continuously building skills and expertise. They value stability and security, and are well-suited for process-oriented environments and roles that allow them to work with accuracy and precision.

Common jobs for people with the Dc personality type are:

- Product manager

- Operations manager

- Operations director

- Chief operating officer

- Attorney

- Project manager

- Architect

- Sales operations manager

- Finance director

HOW TO USE YOUR PERSONALITY TO YOUR ADVANTAGE

By now, you should have a solid idea of which personality type most lines up with your behavior. It's okay if you laughed (or cried) a little bit as you read through the description—many of us do. It's a fun exercise. However, when you understand how your behavior fits into a real, observable model in the world, that's when the ultimate value begins.

In the following chapters, you will learn how to not only identify your personality type and traits, but also how to use your strengths to your advantage and properly manage your blind spots. You will learn how you can best work with other people to create mutually beneficial partnerships. You will learn how to adjust your communication style and address difficult conversations with confidence and ease. And you will learn how to make better decisions for your own personal growth, to the benefit of your career and all of those around you.

Chapter Ten

HOW I FIRED (AND THEN REHIRED) MYSELF

In early 2018, three years after starting Crystal, I officially reached burnout.

If you've been involved in a startup company before, you're familiar with the frantic pace. Every employee has three or four roles, every day brings a new crisis to handle, and the ground you're standing on feels like it shifts beneath your feet. Every month in a startup feels like a year, especially in a high-growth, venture-backed environment. It's a grind, and it's not for everyone, but I can't get enough of it.

Ever since high school, I almost exclusively worked in these kinds of high-intensity environments, where you need to push through long hours of little progress, constantly brushing up against failure. I sold pizza box advertising door-to-door; I dressed up in a cow costume to sell real estate; I spent a summer hopping from apartment to apartment in Boston to exterminate bed bugs.

No, Crystal is not a grind like those other jobs. I sincerely love our company and the people I get to spend my days with. Our mission is one that I have dedicated my whole career to, and one to which I will gladly devote many, many more late nights. Our product is great, and the market is growing. There's a lot to be excited about.

But still, I hit burnout. It wasn't necessarily a physical thing, but a mental one. I didn't want to go into the office; didn't want to meet with anyone; didn't want to sell anything; didn't want to build the product.

After hitting brick wall after brick wall, I simply did not want to think about the company I had started. I felt caught in an endless loop, thinking about the same problems and doing the same mental gymnastics to imagine solutions, only to arrive at the same problems again. I questioned whether I actually wanted to succeed with this company. And that terrified me.

Luckily, I had a business partner to snap me out of this self-defeating loop.

Greg had just started his new role as president and COO, and one of his first orders of business was "fixing" me. He saw that my personal burnout was one of the biggest risks for the company, so as one would expect from an *Architect (Dc)* personality type, he needed to perform CEO surgery. And boy, did it make a difference.

DIAGNOSING THE CAUSES OF STRESS, INEFFECTIVENESS, AND BURNOUT

First, Greg needed to identify and understand the symptoms that the company and I were experiencing:

- Inability to follow through on major initiatives to bring them to completion.

- Many new ideas and plans, but lack of organization to execute them.

- Inefficient processes and unclear responsibilities among the team.

- General stagnation in upward progress.

As DISC practitioners, we could see a clear pattern here. My natural personality type is *Id* (the *Influencer*), and we were seeing some of the results of an *I* culture running rampant without enough *C* to balance it out. Blind spots were allowed to grow, unchecked, into giant caverns.

Next, we wrote out each job that I had. We defined a *job* as something that took a significant amount of my time each month (see the list in Table 10.1), which would ordinarily be a full-time role at a much larger company.

Table 10.1 Drew's jobs at Crystal.

JOB	% OF DREW'S TIME
Direct sales (meetings, calls, emails)	20%
Admin (HR, accounting, legal, etc.)	10%
Sales and marketing management	10%
Customer support	10%
Team management	10%
Product management	10%
Product design and content	10%
Product strategy	5%
Marketing strategy	5%
Company strategy	5%
PR (investor relations, media, etc.)	5%

If that seems like a lot, it's because it is. Now, I wish I could tell you that I am the type of rockstar CEO who can accomplish all of these simultaneously. But what actually happened was paralysis. I had spread myself so thin that I wasn't doing *any* of them well. Merely keeping my head above water was exhausting.

But as we dug into this more, we realized that it was far worse than being spread too thin.

THE HIDDEN COST OF TRYING TO BE THE HERO

It wasn't just the high volume of jobs; it was the insane variety of them. On any given day, I would need to hop from "peppy sales guy" to "firm task driver" to "analytical spreadsheet wizard." We plotted out each job on the Personality Map to see where the dots were, relative to my own personality (see Figure 10.1).

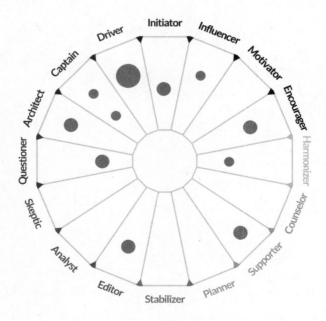

Figure 10.1 The Personality Map showing all of Drew's jobs.

Bingo.

While my "home" was way up in the *Influencer (Id)* region, I was routinely driving across the map to regions like *Analyst (C), Architect (Dc)*, and *Stabilizer (SC)*. In terms of the energy cost that we discussed before, that's a way to guzzle a ton of gas in a hurry.

And the more time I spent far away from home, slaying Excel dragons and fighting fires with our engineering team, the less time I could spend *at* home focusing on the work that I actually enjoyed. This happens to be the work I can actually do really well with enough focus—product design, content writing, prototyping, and so on.

None of this was rocket science. It was just shocking to see it all at once. The answer of "how to fix Drew" was right in front of us on that white board.

Greg drew a smaller circle within the map, around my dot (see Figure 10.2). He said, "Everything inside this circle should be your job, and we should eliminate or delegate everything outside the circle."

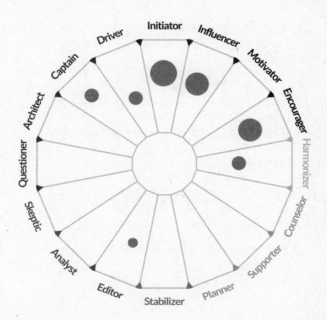

Figure 10.2 The Personality Map showing only the jobs Drew should keep.

If I could reduce the amount of time I spent *far away from home*, and maximize the time I spent *close to home*, we could see a path to launch me out of this season of burnout. The goal was to double down on my strengths (the traits that give me an unfair advantage over most people) and manage my blind spots (the traits that make me less effective than most people).

DOUBLING DOWN ON STRENGTHS

Once we understood some of the underlying causes of personality differences, we were able to see our minds like a car. We can get behind the wheel of any functioning automobile and drive it *most* places, but every car is designed for a different purpose. Some are built to optimize for speed along a smooth, straight freeway, while others are built to climb mountains. Some are built for fuel-efficiency, others for hauling power.

To fix my burnout problem, I needed to start driving my car in better ways, more in line with what it was built for. For example, as an *Influencer (Id)*, it comes very naturally for me to:

- Initiate conversations with new people.

- Improvise in situations where I need to think on my feet.

- Introduce people to new ideas and new people.

- Develop new solutions and strategies without much structure or process.

- Work across multiple disciplines and build new skill sets.

MANAGING BLIND SPOTS

In my everyday job, however, I was committing far more time to my blind spots. These include:

- Delegating responsibilities to the team in an efficient way.

- Creating rules and processes for others to follow.

- Keeping people organized, on task, and on time.

- Accounting for all of the logistics and potential risks involved with a change.

In these areas, it took a tremendous amount of energy for me to perform at an average level, so most of the time I was either mediocre or ineffective. Worse still, all that energy I was committing to the blind spots was stealing the energy and time that could be devoted to the strengths. So, rather than getting outsized returns from my unfair competitive advantages, those strengths were actually brought back down to *just good enough to get by*. That's not how I wanted to run my company or my career.

STAYING CLOSE TO HOME

Now, I happen to be lucky that most of the jobs I struggled with are actually the areas in which Greg is uniquely gifted. The man decorates his desk with Quarterly Objectives, he treats the paper shredder like his pet, and he has never met a Trello board he didn't like. So, many of my weaker responsibilities could go directly to him, and the others could be thoughtfully dispersed among better-suited people on the team.

At the end of this exercise, we set targets for how I should be spending my time (see Table 10.2).

With this activity breakdown as a guide, I made some dramatic adjustments to my daily routine and set up guardrails for what I *should* and *should not* be doing. Previously, my day included "whatever the company happens to need right now."

Table 10.2 Drew's revised job list.

JOB	TIME
Product strategy	30%
Product design and content	20%
Marketing strategy	20%
Direct sales (meetings, calls, emails)	10%
Company strategy	10%
PR (investor relations, media, etc.)	5%
Admin (HR, accounting, legal, etc.)	5%
Customer support	0%
Sales and marketing management	0%
Team management	0%
Product management	0%

I gave up control over most processes, management, and organization to Greg. I dove deep into strategy, design, and communication, shifting my schedule *away* from structured blocks of meetings and *toward* long stretches of uninterrupted production. I let go of the impulse to achieve Inbox Zero every day, spent more time in spontaneous customer conversations, and focused on clarifying our company's long-term vision.

One year after this exercise, Crystal is humming.

THE MULTIPLIER EFFECT

Since I let go of the jobs that were *far away from home* and made a strict, intentional effort to focus on the creativity-oriented jobs that are *close to home*, my personal productivity has multiplied, and more important, I can lead the company with energy and excitement for the future.

Greg is also experiencing this multiplier effect. Since he is able to stay close to *his* home with management and process-oriented jobs, he can spend his time directing others, setting deadlines, and organizing tasks—things he does with less energy and much higher effectiveness than anyone else. When presented with a good strategy, he can execute it like a machine.

Furthermore, we took this same exercise and applied it to the whole business. We wanted everyone to spend *most* of their time doing things that required the *lowest* energy cost. It sounds like common sense, but it was amazing how misaligned many of our delegated tasks were. This energy-oriented thinking allows a group to work more efficiently by putting each member into positions where they are most likely to thrive.

The results have been abundantly clear. In addition to simply *feeling* better about our work, our increased productivity as individuals has directly correlated with rapid revenue growth, product innovation, and a much healthier bottom line.

With this little exercise last year, we used personality data to apply *Moneyball* thinking to Crystal, and we are now reaping the benefits. All this information was common sense, once we had a way to visualize it. When you keep people *close to home* most of the time and ask them to drive *far away* less often, they stay energized and thrive.

What made us even more excited was that we could then build this thinking into our own product and help other teams do the same thing.

PART III

How Personality AI Works

Understanding the technology driving
the personality revolution

Chapter Eleven

WHY THE SOFT SKILLS ARE THE HARDEST

Communication, relationship-building, and leadership are typically referred to as "soft skills," but they are often the most difficult to master. And in our hyper-connected modern economy, they are often the prerequisites to authority, influence, and wealth.

Professionals in sales, marketing, recruiting, management, and other people-focused roles know how important communication is to their personal success. When your money comes from your ability to build trust, negotiate effectively, resolve conflicts, and influence others, you pay attention to the way you speak and write. While outreach-oriented jobs can be grinding, they can also be immensely rewarding, with unlimited upside, if you can figure out how to drive others to take action with some degree of predictability. Sometimes, the rewards for a single successful conversation can often wipe away the losses from hundreds (or thousands) of rejections.

So, in the global, hyper-connected knowledge economy, millions of professional communicators are chasing after the same thing—*successful conversations*. With so many people seeking those conversations, however, we have created some real challenges.

Over the past two decades, the Internet has made it easier than ever to reach new people. Social networks have made the world smaller and more transparent, and if we're plugged in, we are more accessible.

In the sales world, *social selling*—the strategy of connecting with prospects and building customer relationships through social media channels—has become standard practice. In addition, business development has become an extremely technology-driven process, as new platforms have emerged to make reps more efficient by automating as much outreach as possible.

The recruiting world has undergone a similar transformation, as staffing firms and internal talent departments who are incentivized by placements seek to reach as many candidates, as fast as possible. With the help of talent acquisition software platforms, the best-qualified candidates are routinely inundated with opportunities to change jobs via their own social profiles.

This holds true inside companies, as well. As leaders grow more dependent on email and messaging platforms for internal communication, they face the same stiff competition for their employees' attention. With so much extra noise, it's easier than ever for messages to get lost in the shuffle.

HOW TECHNOLOGY CREATES COMMUNICATION CHALLENGES

The explosion of electronic outreach has certainly provided benefits (we all still use email and social media), but it has created a serious economic problem for professional communicators: we have reduced the cost of communicating to almost zero.

When communication is so cheap, the demand for attention grows exponentially. Since the supply of attention stays roughly the same, your attention becomes far more valuable.

As a consumer, I'm in a seller's market for my attention, and I can afford to be skeptical. I will simply ignore most messages until I get one that is *extremely* relevant to me.

Advertising, sales, recruiting, and media are industries that are all fueled by attention, and this new paradigm has already blown them up. While in the past, the voice with the loudest megaphone could overwhelm the others and conquer a winner-take-all market for attention, that's simply no longer the case. Instead, the companies and individuals that rise to the top of these industries are the ones who have the best information to achieve *relevance* and effectively use that information to add value in every interaction.

Think about how Netflix disrupted film distribution with a personalized, on-demand watching experience. Or how Amazon continues to conquer new markets with a relentless obsession with giving customers exactly what they want. Or how Google and Facebook Ads have taken over a massive percentage of marketing spend by delivering hyper-targeted ads in a dramatically more efficient way than was ever before possible.

In a hyper-connected, hyper-skeptical world, the winners are the people and organizations who understand their audience better than anyone else. In a word, they use *empathy*.

HOW TECHNOLOGY CAN SOLVE COMMUNICATION CHALLENGES

Machine learning, combined with the explosion of data available to analyze, has now made it possible to map out how people think and behave at scale, allowing us to better understand our customers, colleagues, and connections. This new approach to communication is called *Personality AI*. With technology-enabled empathy, people can accelerate trust, build relationships, and win more business in a world that is noisier and less trusting than ever before.

Personality AI sits at the intersection of three converging trends:

1. *Personality psychology* has taken off in popularity and advanced significantly in scientific validity. Individuals and businesses are using personality models to understand each other and achieve better outcomes.

2. *Social networks* have exploded and enabled us to publish all kinds of information that our friends, coworkers, and connections can access to learn about us.

3. *Machine learning* has progressed to the point where computers can cost-effectively analyze large amounts of data, identify trends, and make highly confident predictions about future results.

At our company, Crystal, we first brought Personality AI to market in 2015. Since then, we have seen both the technology and adoption advance tremendously, as early adopters have used our products for millions of emails, meetings, and phone calls with amazing results that they often refer to as "magic."

In *The 7 Habits of Highly Effective People*, Stephen Covey said, "Seek First to Understand, Then to Be Understood." This principle is as old as humanity, but when you combine it with the new technologies and datasets that we have access to in the modern world, the result *feels* magical. Human connection is mysterious, but when you *click* with someone, you know it.

In the following chapters, we will explain how Personality AI helps you click with more people, more frequently, especially when you communicate for a living. You will learn about the possibilities it opens up, how it works under the hood, and how you can use it to accelerate your own career. Since we are still in the very early stages of this emerging market, the early adopters are the ones who can gain the greatest advantage.

Our society encourages people to build digital walls around their attention, and it can be incredibly draining to run into them, headfirst, day after day. That's what modern communication often feels like, but there is another way. Our mission is to use data, technology, and ancient wisdom to help people break through the walls with empathy and connect with others with much more success.

By accurately and quickly understanding each other's personalities, we can build a future where relationships are more trusting, more productive, and ultimately, more meaningful.

Chapter Twelve

BEFORE PERSONALITY AI: FLYING BLIND

With such important information about a person's style, preferences, motivations, strengths, and blind spots, personality profiles are very useful for one-on-one communication. These traits are real, they are profound, and they can help to create powerful connections between people.

There is a problem, though: historically, there have only been a few ways to accurately and measurably understand someone's personality:

- Get to know them personally, over a long period of time.

- Ask many people who know them about their personality and find the commonalities.

- Have them complete a personality test and allow you to read the results.

But what about the *billions* of other people who you don't know?

Because of the built-in limitations of assessments, personality data is simply unavailable for most people. In your limited time, you can only meet so many people; and in a company with limited resources, you can only get so many participants in a personality study.

As a result, personality assessments are typically confined to the realm of human resources, management consulting, and training. The amount of personality profiles you can access is limited to the number of people you can rope into a group exercise, and even then, each person must dedicate precious time to answer questions accurately. Even after the most engaging, productive, conversation-stimulating session of personality assessments and communication training, most participants tend to leave with a feeling of "that was fun," and continue on with their jobs without the chance to apply their lessons.

Lots of professionals—like those in sales, marketing, recruiting, and other communication-oriented roles—spend most of their day talking to total strangers. Their objective is usually to convince these strangers to take some kind of meaningful action, like to spend their money on a new product, or to quit their job and try something new. It's hard work, and it's getting harder.

Most of these communication professionals are flying blind during the most crucial moments of their prospect and customer interactions. In those first few emails, meetings, or phone calls, when it's most important to make a good impression, that's when they unfortunately have the least data available. The gap in knowledge leads to a gap in *empathy*.

With more information before interactions, you can make each of them more effective and data-driven, rather than gut-driven. This is where the personality revolution has its most immediate impact.

Chapter Thirteen

HOW AI IS ALREADY IMPACTING YOU

AI seems to be everywhere now, and with good reason. Our modern lifestyles produce massive amounts of data—from what we search for, where we drive, what we eat, what we watch, and other daily choices. Companies have discovered powerful, creative ways to use that data for our benefit.

In the past decade, AI has exploded in growth as innovators have built powerful consumer products that harness the technology. Perhaps the most well-known examples are AI assistants, such as Siri and Alexa. Despite some privacy concerns and several hiccups since these products have been brought to market, millions of people are getting firsthand experience with AI in their daily lives. These AI assistants are changing the way we perform ordinary daily tasks like checking the weather, playing music, setting reminders, and even learning knock-knock jokes.

In addition to assistants, AI bots are becoming common in the business world. Microsoft Azure has a service that allows companies to build powerful, smart AI bots for interacting with customers through online chat, making the customer experience smoother and faster.[1] Upstarts like HubSpot and Drift have similar services for any size company to

---

[1] Azure Bot Service, https://azure.microsoft.com/en-us/services/bot-service.

launch a chatbot on their website without writing any code. These AI bots are qualifying prospects, booking sales demos, and ultimately helping people get quicker answers.

While assistants and bots are the most common applications of AI you might see in action, the technology is also impacting our lives less directly in more under the hood ways. A fantastic example is recommendation engines. Amazon is an industry leader in this area, with product recommendations that are personalized for every customer based on buying history, browsing habits, and preferences. Netflix and Spotify have advanced engines for video and music, respectively. These engines help us discover new movies and songs that we are likely to enjoy.

These applications of AI are merely the beginning. The technology has tremendous potential in critical areas such as medicine, defense, finance, and more. At the 2018 World Economic Forum, Salesforce chairman and CEO Marc Benioff referred to AI as a "new human right." He proclaimed that "those who have artificial intelligence will be smarter, will be healthier, and will be richer."[2] Conversely, those without it will be "weaker and poorer, less educated and sicker."

AI FOR COMMUNICATION

There is a new class of AI that helps people communicate better. A prime example is Salesforce Einstein, dubbed as "AI for Everyone," which provides powerful AI tools that help companies understand the sentiment and intent of customer communication within their CRM (customer relationship management). Other companies like Cogito provide tools for support call centers using Emotional AI. This technology provides customer support representatives with emotional sentiment and other insights while they are on the phone with customers, helping them deliver a more personalized, satisfying customer experience.

[2] Rosalie Chan, "Salesforce CEO Marc Benioff Calls Artificial Intelligence a 'New Human Right,'" *Business Insider*, January 23, 2019, https://www.businessinsider.com/salesforces-benioff-calls-artificial-intelligence-a-new-human-right-2019-1.

Personality AI is a fast-growing segment of this new class of AI for communication. IBM's Watson helped pioneer this development using text sample analysis to identify the personality of a company's customers. Crystal maps millions of personality-related data points and uses them in text-sample analysis to identify the personality of customers, prospects, and employees.

Of all the currently available AI applications, Personality AI is perhaps the most human-centric. Behavior is often unpredictable, and relationships are complex, so it takes a lot of data to find patterns and apply models that are accurate enough to be useful. In the next chapter, we will go into detail about the underlying concepts and technologies that make Personality AI possible, and how it is rapidly developing to be more powerful in the near future.

Chapter Fourteen

A GPS FOR COMMUNICATING WITH PEOPLE

Before we get into the details of understanding customers and personalizing our communication for them, it's important to understand the "AI" part of Personality AI at a base level.

AI, or artificial intelligence, is a very broad term that frequently gets thrown around boardrooms, living rooms, and tech conferences without many specifics. It's an easy basket to throw buzzwords into—like "big data," "machine learning," "natural language processing," "voice recognition," or "predictive analytics." Too often, it's used as a way to fudge over some poor CTO's missing details in a PowerPoint presentation.

For our purposes, we are going with Andreas Kaplan's definition:[1]

Artificial Intelligence (AI)—defined as a system's ability to correctly interpret external data, to learn from such data, and to use those learnings to achieve specific goals and tasks . . .

[1] "Siri, Siri, in my hand: Who's the fairest in the land? On the interpretations, illustrations, and implications of artificial intelligence," *Business Horizons* 62 (2019): 15–25, https://app .dimensions.ai/details/publication/pub.1108035135?and_facet_journal=jour.1122304.

AI has widespread applications. It powers Facebook's photo-tagging facial recognition,[2] Tesla's self-driving autopilot system,[3] Netflix's content recommendation engine,[4] and thousands of other products that are already impacting your life. Personality AI is an extremely targeted use of this technology to understand how specific people are likely to behave, communicate, and respond to external forces.

We have been using the Personality Map as our guide to understand behavior in a structured way and confidently navigate relationships. Personality AI is the GPS system to the Personality Map. It's like using Google Maps (instead of a paper one) to get around a city.

WHY PERSONALITY AI IS REVOLUTIONARY ⎯⎯⎯

Personality AI can provide insights about a person's behavior without a traditional personality assessment, and that opens up an entirely new world of possibilities for communicating and interacting with others, such as:

- Accelerating trust and openness between people who are speaking to each other for the first time.

- Helping professionals write emails in a style that their recipients read and enjoy, rather than ignore.

- Understanding the relational dynamics that two people are likely to experience when they work together.

---

[2] Yaniv Taingman, Ming Yang, Marc'Aurelio Ranzato, and Lior Wolf, "DeepFace: Closing the Gap to Human-Level Performance in Face Verification," Conference on Computer Vision and Pattern Recognition (CVPR), June 24, 2014, https://research.fb.com/publications/deepface-closing-the-gap-to-human-level-performance-in-face-verification.
[3] Kyle Field, "Tesla Director of AI Discusses Programming a Neural Net for Autopilot," CleanTechnica, June 11, 2018, https://cleantechnica.com/2018/06/11/tesla-director-of-ai-discusses-programming-a-neural-net-for-autopilot-video.
[4] Allen Yu, "How Netflix Uses AI and Machine Learning," Becoming Human, February 27, 2019, https://becominghuman.ai/how-netflix-uses-ai-and-machine-learning-a087614630fe.

- Matching people with roles and tasks that are well-aligned with their personality and give them energy.

This new technology is only possible with the recent convergence of abundant data, machine learning, and modern personality theory. As it continues to develop and work its way into new industries, it has the power to make all kinds of professional interactions more personalized and effective.

THE PERSONALITY ALGORITHM

To understand how Personality AI works, we can look at it like a decision-making machine. For every decision, we have a set of inputs, a way to judge those inputs, and a process for coming up with an expected output.

Imagine you're visiting a new restaurant for the first time, and it's your turn to order. How do you decide?

Surely, you don't select a random item. Your choice depends on many different data points:

- What have you liked or disliked in the past?

- What ingredients have given you an allergic reaction in the past?

- What are your friends recommending?

- What time of the day is it?

- What did you eat last night?

- How hungry are you right now?

Your brain (the *original* AI) crunches all of those numbers subconsciously and chooses the meal with the *highest probability of success*. You probably don't even know how you did most of those calculations, or which variables came into play, but the computation happened and you arrived at an answer.

AI works like that, except it can analyze thousands or millions of data points and be applied to any kind of problem, regardless of your individual, personal experience. As long as you have a dataset and enough computational power to analyze it, you can make a prediction with AI.

To be sure, AI is not a magic potion to solve the world's problems. It is fraught with risks and inaccuracies, and it often suffers from the same biases that lead humans to make bad decisions. In fact, many of our oldest truisms about human behavior can be applied just as well to AI, like *garbage in, garbage out.*

When it is used properly, however, AI can be an incredibly powerful tool to make predictions and calculated guesses about *things that you do not know for sure*. Personality AI, specifically, aims to understand someone's typical behavioral patterns as accurately as possible, and uses that information to help you communicate with them more effectively.

Personality AI takes multiple types of input—questionnaire responses, text samples, demographic data, real-life observations—and outputs personality insights (see Figure 14.1). These insights can be descriptions about my own behavior or advice for interacting with other people (whether or not I already know them).

For most people, the value of Personality AI is in the output, which usually comes in the form of personalized advice for navigating a particular situation. Tools like Crystal, for example, provide insights like "how to best communicate," "what motivates this person," and "how to write an email" to help them understand the people they work with and

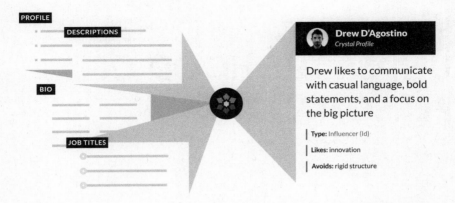

Figure 14.1 Personality AI takes inputs like text samples and outputs personality insights.

communicate more effectively with them. With on-demand insights like this, they can make Personality AI a routine part of their daily meetings, phone calls, and emails.

As someone reading this book, however, you are probably more curious about *how* these insights are generated. To understand the inner workings of Personality AI, it helps to touch on the basic elements of personality theory, data science, and machine learning. In the following chapters, we will dive into each of those areas, as well as the most impactful ways you can start applying Personality AI in your career.

Although Crystal and other companies have pioneered this technology in recent years, it is still in its early stages of adoption. As someone who understands how it works and how to use it, you will be sailing with a GPS while most of your peers and competitors are still navigating by the stars.

Chapter Fifteen
UNDER THE HOOD OF PERSONALITY AI

Ever since building the first prototype of Crystal, it has provided incredible fodder for dinner party conversations.

"So what do you do?"

"I started a software company called Crystal."

"What does the software do?"

"It's an app that tells you anyone's personality."

"What? How does it do that?"

At that point, we usually offer to find the person's personality profile on the spot and let them read it. More than 80% of the time, Crystal produces extremely accurate insights about their communication style, motivations, and behavior. Then the person insists that we look up their spouse/boss/ex, and their jaw drops (especially when they see relationship-oriented insights).

It's fun for us to briefly play the part of Digital Wizard as Crystal gains another fan, but after they see a few more profiles, most people only have more questions . . .

How was it so accurate?

Where does Crystal get the data?

Is this like a horoscope?

Can I do this myself?

Who can see this?

You may have some of those questions now, as well. While this is not a technical manual, I think it is useful to have some basic knowledge about what is going on under the hood of Personality AI before you start using it in your job. In this chapter, we will cover the specific goals of this technology, what the limitations are, and how it improves over time. With a solid foundation, you can better understand how to use it properly and what to expect in the future.

Many of these concepts are universal for any artificial intelligence, and you can often apply the same patterns of thinking to different problems. Personality AI is a narrow, yet powerful use case for the technology. It is particularly exciting to us because of how large the potential audience is, and how many relationships it can improve between real people.

ACCURACY VERSUS CONVENIENCE

The goal of Personality AI is to identify someone's behavioral patterns as accurately as possible, which is usually represented by a personality type or a set of specific personality traits. With that information, it can power tools that facilitate more effective communication, stronger relationships, and better decision-making.

We want to highlight the phrase *as accurately as possible*. We're not looking to identify personality types as *conveniently* as possible, or as *quickly* as possible. The first goal is accuracy, and then all of the business benefits come after that.

In some cases, the most accurate methods are not available, so we need to make a trade-off between accuracy and convenience. Convenience can mean getting a personality profile *faster*, generating it with *less data*, or not needing another person to participate.

The three primary methods for identifying someone's personality are assessments, text sample analysis, and attribute analysis. As discussed earlier in this book, each method has its own trade-offs (see Table 15.1).

Table 15.1 Methods for identifying a person's personality.

METHOD	BENEFITS	FLAWS
Assessments	• High accuracy. • Widespread familiarity and acceptance.	• Time-consuming. • Susceptible to manipulation and bias from the person. • Requires participation from the person.

(continued)

Table 15.1 (*continued*)

METHOD	BENEFITS	FLAWS
Text-sample analysis	• Reliable accuracy. • Fast and convenient for individual analysis. • Does not require participation from the person.	• Requires sufficient text samples from the person. • Susceptible to inaccuracy from people who intentionally modify their writing style.
Attribute analysis	• Only scalable method for analyzing large groups. • Makes predictions possible with limited data. • Does not require participation from the person.	• Only moderate accuracy, especially with small number of attributes. • Requires structured dataset.

ASSESSMENTS

Traditional questionnaire-style assessments are still the most reliably accurate measurement of personality. Therefore, we want to use them whenever possible, particularly in situations when:

- You are making important decisions with the data that may impact a person's career, relationships, or lifestyle.

- You are using the data to support a long-term relationship, rather than a single conversation.

- The person is available and willing to fill out an assessment.

Once someone completes a personality assessment on a platform like Crystal, they can make their profile available to anyone who needs it. A validated, reliable assessment result can be considered the gold standard for understanding their personality archetype until additional evidence proves otherwise.

How Personality Assessments Work

If you have taken many questionnaire-style personality assessments over the course of your career, you have probably noticed that they are structured differently. Some contain simple multiple-choice questions, others ask you to sort or rank a large list of words, and others require you to provide numeric ratings for a set of different behaviors, indicating how much or how little it sounds like *you*.

Regardless of the mechanism, these assessments are all aiming to accomplish the same thing—accurately identify a personality type from a standardized set of responses. Valid assessments are built from a set of responses that come from a random, statistically significant population. A data analyst can plot the responses on a model and see where they tend to cluster together (usually around similar types of behavior), and then create a label to identify each of the behavioral clusters. The label is the "personality type" and it can then be tested against new assessments, future versions of the same assessment, and real-world behavior.

Different personality assessments measure behaviors and personality traits differently. For example, a Big Five assessment will report each of a respondent's five traits (Openness, Conscientiousness, Extraversion, Agreeableness, Neuroticism) as a percentile of the general population (90% Conscientiousness means you are more conscientious than 90% of the population). DISC, on the other hand, typically reports a behavioral pattern than can be visualized on a chart (very high D, high I, low S, very low C) and shortened to a label ("Di").

Crystal detects DISC profiles with a forced-choice word assessment and plots the results on a circular disc-like chart, broken up into the 16 personality types. The assessment requires that respondents select the words that are "most like me" and "least like me" from 14 sets of 4 words. After completing it, everyone has a dot, representing the average position of each of their responses. The region where that dot falls can tell you the most likely personality type. With this short questionnaire, we are able to consistently achieve accuracy confidence above 95%.

Problems with Personality Assessments

While they are the most accurate and consistent method for identifying personality types, assessments are susceptible to biases that can harm their validity. The most universal of these is known as *social desirability bias*.

Personality types are generally neutral in their results, meaning that there is no type that is better than another, and there is no "right" answer to a personality assessment. Social desirability bias comes into play when a person unintentionally or intentionally responds in a way that they perceive to be more desirable, rather than a way that truly reflects how they behave.

This could happen for a number of reasons:

- They may think an employer is looking for a specific personality type for a job.

- They may perceive some responses as being *better* than others. For example, being "friendly" or "ambitious" or "detail-oriented" is generally good, despite the correlations with different personality types.

- There may be strong cultural associations with certain behaviors that other cultures do not share. For example, being "direct" may have a positive connotation in corporate America, but a negative one in Japan.

Social desirability is mostly an unintentional bias, and it can creep into any self-assessment. In developing the Crystal personality assessment, we consistently need to validate the questions, work to detect bias in the responses, and *normalize* the results (i.e. adjust the results into a normal "bell curve" distribution).

For example, our first assessment had the word "aggressive" as a response to one of the questions. Users were prompted to select the word that best described them, as well as the word that least described them.

This was the set of options:

- Organized

- Aggressive

- Positive

- Cooperative

This is called a forced-choice questionnaire. Since we are using DISC as a base, each response aligns with a particular DISC type. In a perfect world, 25% of people would select each option, according to their primary DISC type.

Of course, real life is never as clean as the theory, so an assessment needs to ask lots of questions, continuing to collect responses until it reveals a pattern. There are many factors and biases that can influence any particular selection, so the assessment needs to keep asking questions to tease out those biases. In this question, we saw a very strong social desirability bias after a few thousand people took the assessment, significantly impacting the overall results.

This version of the assessment expected *D*-types to select "Aggressive" as *most like them* and *S*-types to select "Aggressive" as *least like them*. The *I*-types and *C*-types were expected to have a roughly even spread.

However, the data showed that *every type* selected "Aggressive" as *least like them*. While it is technically a behavior associated with *D*-types, it turns out that nobody (not even a *D*-type) likes to view themselves as aggressive, at least when there are other options available. This is likely a result of negative cultural and social connotations. While we sometimes view aggressiveness as a positive (like when a basketball player weaves through a crowded floor and scores), the more negative meanings (like a schoolyard bully who won't stop pestering kids on the playground) override our overall sentiment. As a result, the word is nearly meaningless in an assessment and skews most of the results farther away from *D*-types than they should be.

In hindsight, we probably could have predicted the social desirability bias that we saw with the word "Aggressive" and revised the assessment before releasing the first version. However, these biases are not always obvious. The following is another example that would have been very hard to detect on instinct alone.

That same assessment included this option set for one of the questions:

- Cautious

- Energetic

- Engaging

- Satisfied

We originally expected that respondents with *C*-type personalities (Editors, Analysts, Skeptics, Questioners) would select "Cautious" as one of their dominant characteristics. However, after several thousand assessments, the data told a different story.

In fact, *C*-types actually selected "Cautious" as *least like them* about 20% more often than they selected it as *most like them!* This was totally contradictory to our initial assumption.

It was the *S*-types (Counselors, Supporters, Planners, Stabilizers) who selected it far more often than everyone else. Why was this the case? We can only speculate. But we could verify with a high degree of certainty that there was a bias that *S*-types had toward self-reported cautiousness, and we could use that knowledge to adjust our assessment and detect *S*-types more confidently.

Beyond individual responses, social desirability bias can affect the overall results of an assessment, and needs to be corrected on a global level rather than question by question. In the case of the Crystal assessment, our response data consistently reveals distinct trends within job titles, countries, and industries. These are useful, and we will get into how they are helpful for making personality predictions later in the chapter.

However, when we look at the response data as a whole, we see that the average respondent always *shades* toward the right side of the Personality Map. In other words, people answer questions in a way that makes them seem like slightly more of an *I*-type or an *S*-type. This cannot be boiled down to individual questions, but more of a cultural bias toward seeing yourself as a friendly, kind person.

When these biases are extremely strong (like in the case of being labeled as "aggressive"), sometimes entire questions need to be tossed out or replaced. When the biases are more subtle (like with "being cautious" or the *I*-type/*S*-type tendency), the assessment results can be normalized. It's only possible after thousands, or hundreds of thousands of responses. Assessments need to be battle-tested, validated, and adjusted to handle bias.

We could go into much more detail with this, but here are the important takeaways:

- Personality assessments are susceptible to unconscious social biases that can skew the results, especially when they purely rely on the respondent to describe themselves.

- Personality assessment responses are not always intuitive, and they may not align with personality types in the way you expect.

- You should only trust personality assessments that have normalized, validated results to account for biases.

Limitations of Personality Assessments

There are times when questionnaire-style personality assessments are not feasible. This is true for most outreach scenarios, as well as situations when:

- You do not know the other person, or they are not available to complete a personality assessment.

- You are only using the data for a short-term purpose, like an email or a phone conversation.

- You are not using the data in a way that has a material impact on the other person, such as a job placement or team assignment.

In these kinds of situations, Personality AI can help us make personality predictions *without* the other person completing an assessment. By using machine learning along with the person-level data that is available to us, Personality AI unlocks two entirely new approaches to improving our communication and relationships.

TEXT-SAMPLE ANALYSIS

The first non-assessment method for identifying personality is *text-sample analysis*. This technique uses natural language processing (NLP) and machine learning (ML) to detect someone's personality type by analyzing an unstructured sample of text that they authored.

The text can come from many sources, including:

- Social media profiles

- Online bios and articles

- Resumés

- Emails and direct messages

- Website reviews and comments

With a sufficiently sized text sample, a well-trained machine learning algorithm can predict someone's personality type with a surprising level of accuracy (Crystal's text-sample predictions have been consistently measured above 80%). This type of analysis provides a solid option for anyone looking to use personality data in customer outreach.

How Text-Sample Analysis Works

Natural language processing is a broad field, encompassing many applications like voice-to-text transcription, sentiment analysis, author identity, and more. In Personality AI, we are using it specifically to detect the *personality type of the person who wrote a text sample*.

While it can get quite complicated, at the most basic level we can view any text sample in the same way we view a personality assessment. Every word that someone writes is a specific *choice* they make to express an idea, just like the options they select in a personality assessment. Because text samples are so unstructured, it takes a lot more written words than assessment responses to detect the trends, but the trends are there nonetheless.

The most straightforward way to detect a personality type from a text sample is from n-gram analysis. In computer science, a "gram" is a sequence of items that we can count in a block of text. It could be letters, words, punctuation marks, groups of words, or more. In our case, we are using groups of one, two, and three words—known as *unigrams*, *bigrams*, and *trigrams*.

When you have a training set of thousands (or millions) of text samples, along with valid personality assessments, you can detect the differences in writing style and content across personality types. This is especially true when you are using a more structured set of samples, like resumés or social media profiles.

Some n-grams, like "customers" or "managed a team," do not reveal any significant patterns. They are used roughly equally, or randomly, by each personality type and as a result they tell you very little about the author of any given text sample. Other n-grams, however, have strong correlations with personality, and can tell you a lot about the person. Here are some notable examples from the Crystal data:

- "Return on investment" has a strong correlation with *D*-types.

- "Plain awesome" has a strong correlation with *I*-types.

- "Weekly meetings" has a strong correlation with *S*-types.

- "Continuously evaluated" has a strong correlation with *C*-types.

There is a nearly infinite number of n-grams that a person can choose to write, and it would be impossible to understand the exact amount that each one reveals about a personality trait. However, we don't need to understand the impact of every word to get a highly confident personality prediction. All we need to do is get a statistically large enough sample of n-grams—ideally in many different sentences and contexts—to start seeing patterns. Those patterns can then be applied to a Personality AI algorithm to detect personality types even more quickly and accurately from future text samples.

Problems with Text-Sample Analysis

Just like personality assessments, text-sample analysis is not immune to bias and has several flaws of its own.

One major issue is identity. When analyzing a text sample, it is most helpful if you can verify that it was written by the person you think it was written by. Otherwise, you may be detecting the personality of another person, or even a content-producing bot, which can influence the result (although, you can still usually draw conclusions effectively from a sample written *about* a person).

Even if you have the right author, the person may write in a way that does not reflect their true personality. Social desirability bias affects how we present ourselves, especially in a professional or public context. I may try to craft my personal brand as an intense, forceful, high-energy *Captain (D)* on my LinkedIn profile, when in reality I'm a warm, supportive *Counselor (Si)*. Personality AI might pick up the incorrect type.

Accuracy comes down to having a large volume of clean, verifiable data to analyze. In some instances, we simply do not have enough of it and need to look for other clues about someone's personality. That brings us to the next method . . .

ATTRIBUTE ANALYSIS

The last method is *attribute analysis*. Instead of text samples written *by* the person, this technique analyzes more structured data *about* the person to make a personality prediction. These attributes can include things like:

- Past and current job titles

- Past and current employers

- Industries in which the person has worked

- Places where the person has lived

- Schools the person has attended

- Interests the person has

- Topics the person has written or posted about

None of these data points can be used individually to make an accurate prediction—people with an interest in "baseball," or who work in "technology," or who are employed by "IBM" certainly do not all have the same personality. However, they can be combined and weighted to tell us where a personality is *most likely* to fall on the Personality Map.

For example, every job title tends to have a personality skew in one direction when you look at personality assessment results in a large enough population. We can only speculate why this happens, and we are not concerned with the *why*. We only want to know what personality types are most common within a particular job title, and how large the disparity is with the least common personality types.

In Table 15.2, we can see that the job title "founder" has some very strong correlations with personality type. Of the thousands of founders who have taken the Crystal personality assessment, over 15% had the *DI* or *Initiator* archetype. The least common was the *Cs* or *Editor* archetype, which made up about 1% of respondents.

If the population of founders was evenly distributed among personality types, we would see each type with 6.25% of the sample. That is far from the case, however, so we can use our personality breakdown to calculate the probability that any given founder has a particular personality archetype (or at least get a closer best guess).

Table 15.2 Personality distribution for the job title "founder."

ARCHETYPE	% POPULATION	PROBABILITY
D (Captain)	8.75%	40% more likely to have the job title "founder"
Di (Driver)	12.59%	101% more likely
DI (Initiator)	15.23%	144% more likely
Id (Influencer)	13.31%	113% more likely
I (Motivator)	11.27%	80% more likely
Is (Encourager)	5.88%	6% less likely
IS (Harmonizer)	4.68%	25% less likely
Si (Counselor)	3.84%	39% less likely
S (Supporter)	5.88%	6% less likely
Sc (Planner)	2.64%	58% less likely
SC (Stabilizer)	3.48%	44% less likely
Cs (Editor)	1.2%	80% less likely
C (Analyst)	1.56%	75% less likely

(continued)

Table 15.2 (continued)

ARCHETYPE	% POPULATION	PROBABILITY
Cd (Skeptic)	2.64%	58% less likely
CD (Questioner)	2.76%	56% less likely
Dc (Architect)	4.32%	31% less likely

With 15% of the sample size, we can infer that any given founder is more than twice as likely to be an *Initiator (DI)* than the average respondent. We can also conclude that a founder is 80% less likely to be an *Editor (Cs)*.

If we zoom out a bit, then we can draw some broader, but more confident conclusions. By combining all of the *upper* archetypes (*D* and *I*) and comparing them to all the *lower* archetypes (*S* and *C*), we can see that a founder has a 76% chance of having an archetype on the top half of the Personality Map.

Let's apply this to another job title, like "accountant" (see Table 15.3).

The personality distribution among accountants is very different from the distribution among founders. While 76% of founders were on the top half of the Personality Map, only 25% of accountants were on the top half.

The population of accountants is dominated by *S*-types, like *Supporters (S)* and *Planners (Sc)*. Very few accountants have archetypes toward the top of the map, like *Driver (Di)* or *Influencer (Id)*.

In this relatively simple comparison, the breakdown makes intuitive sense. We can make a reasonable assumption that founders are

Table 15.3   Personality distribution for the job title "accountant."

ARCHETYPE	% POPULATION	PROBABILITY
D (Captain)	3.4%	46% less likely to have the job title "accountant"
Di (Driver)	0.7%	90% less likely
Dl (Initiator)	3.0%	52% less likely
Id (Influencer)	1.4%	78% less likely
I (Motivator)	4.8%	24% less likely
Is (Encourager)	2.0%	20% less likely
IS (Harmonizer)	7.5%	67% less likely
Si (Counselor)	8.2%	31% less likely
S (Supporter)	19.7%	216% more likely
Sc (Planner)	9.5%	52% more likely
SC (Stabilizer)	8.8%	41% more likely
Cs (Editor)	8.3%	33% more likely
C (Analyst)	8.8%	41% more likely

(continued)

Table 15.3 *(continued)*

ARCHETYPE	% POPULATION	PROBABILITY
Cd (Skeptic)	3.6%	42% less likely
CD (Questioner)	8.6%	38% more likely
Dc (Architect)	1.7%	73% less likely

more likely to exhibit more assertive, risk-seeking behaviors while accountants are more likely to be cautious, methodical, and risk-averse. Job title happens to be a strong indicator of personality type, while other attributes have weaker (but still useful) correlations.

For example, let's look at "country" (see Table 15.4). Of course, if you only know someone's country you cannot make an accurate prediction of their personality. However, different countries have different cultures, social norms, and behavioral expectations, and when you combine it with other attributes about a person, it can move the needle closer to the truth.

In this example, we can observe that the population of respondents from Canada skew toward *D* and *D/I* personality archetypes. We can only speculate the reason for this, but the important thing to know is that there is a significant, measurable difference when you compare people from Canada with the global population.

India's personality distribution is very different, as most people skew towards *S* and *S/C* archetypes (see Table 15.5). Again, this could be driven by cultural variations, differences in social desirability bias, and other factors.

Table 15.4 Personality distribution for the country "Canada."

ARCHETYPE	% POPULATION	PROBABILITY
D (Captain)	8.65%	38% more likely
Di (Driver)	12.62%	102% more likely
DI (Initiator)	12.34%	97% more likely
Id (Influencer)	11.63%	86% more likely
I (Motivator)	8.51%	36% more likely
Is (Encourager)	5.53%	11% less likely
IS (Harmonizer)	3.26%	48% less likely
Si (Counselor)	4.96%	21% less likely
S (Supporter)	7.23%	16% more likely
Sc (Planner)	5.96%	5% less likely
SC (Stabilizer)	4.68%	25% less likely
Cs (Editor)	3.55%	43% less likely
C (Analyst)	3.40%	46% less likely
Cd (Skeptic)	2.55%	59% less likely

(continued)

Table 15.4 (continued)

ARCHETYPE	% POPULATION	PROBABILITY
CD (Questioner)	2.13%	66% less likely
Dc (Architect)	2.98%	52% less likely

Because the sample sizes are so large and diverse, "country" tends to be a much weaker attribute than a more powerful one like "job title." Attributes like "industry," "employers," and "interests" fall somewhere in between.

When you have a large set of attributes about a person, Personality AI compares the attributes to a larger set of training data, runs the probability calculations instantly, and combines the results into a new personality prediction.

If everything goes as planned, you end up with the personality type that this person is *most likely* to embody.

Now, as you can probably imagine, this style of personality analysis can produce wide variations in accuracy, depending on how much or how little data you have available. With lots of information about a person, you can achieve a more confident result. With only a few attributes, it's much lower.

However, attribute analysis has the enormous benefit of allowing you to instantly make personality predictions for a large group of people. For professionals who need to communicate with large lists of people at once (marketers, business development reps, etc.), this can be a powerful method for improving email campaigns, calls to action, and customer success. It can also be used to understand the overall personality trends

Table 15.5 Personality distribution for the country "India."

ARCHETYPE	% POPULATION	PROBABILITY
D (Captain)	3.75%	40% less likely
Di (Driver)	7.33%	17% more likely
DI (Initiator)	7.68%	23% more likely
Id (Influencer)	5.58%	11% less likely
I (Motivator)	7.07%	13% more likely
Is (Encourager)	7.50%	20% more likely
IS (Harmonizer)	9.51%	52% more likely
Si (Counselor)	8.38%	34% more likely
S (Supporter)	10.99%	76% more likely
Sc (Planner)	10.30%	65% more likely
SC (Stabilizer)	6.98%	12% more likely
Cs (Editor)	4.19%	33% less likely
C (Analyst)	3.40%	46% less likely
Cd (Skeptic)	2.27%	64% less likely

(continued)

Table 15.5 (continued)

ARCHETYPE	% POPULATION	PROBABILITY
CD (Questioner)	2.27%	64% less likely
Dc (Architect)	2.79%	55% less likely

within a group of people for crafting customer personas or brand messaging.

At Crystal, we have implemented all of this functionality into our Google Chrome extension, so you can automatically make the most accurate possible personality predictions based on the available data on a web page.

PERSONALITY AND BEHAVIORAL CHANGES

While it's possible to make accurate predictions about someone's personality at any given moment in time, people are not static. Numerous studies[1] indicate that our personality changes as we age,[2] and the transformation is not always very predictable.

Thus, whenever we generate a personality profile from assessments or machine learning, we cannot consider it the forever truth. It's more of a snapshot about a person's behavioral patterns in the here-and-now, but it may change significantly in a year. These changes may be driven by social maturity, biological development, and environmental factors.

[1] Mathew Harris, Caroline Brett, Wendy Johnson, and Ian Deary, "Personality Stability from Age 14 to Age 77 Years," Psychology and Aging 31, no. 8 (2016): 862–874, https://www.ncbi.nlm.nih.gov/pmc/articles/PMC5144810/.
[2] Brent Roberts and Daniel Mroczek, "Personality Trait Change in Adulthood," Current Directions in Psychology Science 17, no. 1 (2008): 31–35, https://www.ncbi.nlm.nih.gov/pmc/articles/PMC2743415/.

Regardless of the reasons for a change, Personality AI must account for the ever-shifting nature of human personality and behavior if it hopes to achieve its goal of *highest possible accuracy*. Our psychology models need to adapt to be just as flexible as the people they represent.

HOW PERSONALITY AI GETS SMARTER OVER TIME

All personality science is based on observing behavioral trends across a large population of people. If you have assessment results from thousands of people, for example, and you know things like their age, job title, or employer, you have a set of *training data* that can be used to find correlations (trends that repeat themselves with some degree of consistency).

If you find enough of these correlations, you can use that data to *train* a machine learning model, which a computer can use to accurately predict personality profiles in the future. The more data you have, the better the predictions get.

Let's say you are walking around a college campus and you notice something funny when interacting with the students. Whenever you meet a student wearing a red shirt, they seem to be loud, boisterous, and outgoing. Most of them crack jokes, lead the conversation, and ask you lots of questions. However, whenever you meet a student in a blue shirt, they appear more quiet, reserved, and thoughtful. They usually listen closely to what you say and do not interrupt.

Real life isn't usually this clean, but let's oversimplify for the illustration. From your experience, you could make a reasonable judgement that *students in red shirts tend to be more extroverted*, while *students in blue shirts tend to be more introverted*.

Now, this type of thinking can lead to severe, even harmful bias for a few reasons:

- You may have only met a small number of students compared to the whole population, and the fact that some were more or less introverted was a function of random chance, rather than a true correlation (sampling bias).

- There could be other, external factors causing the personality differences you observe. You may have visited the campus on a game day, where one college wears blue and the other wears red to support their team (omitted-variable bias).

- You could be subconsciously approaching people in red shirts with a more outgoing, positive demeanor, leading them in turn to respond in a more extroverted way. In this case, the personality difference may not be shirt color, but the social dynamics that changed their behavior (social desirability bias).

When people or algorithms make decisions without enough training data, or with inherent flaws in their training dataset, they make inaccurate predictions. This is where false positives and incorrect stereotypes come from, and it's why data quality is so crucial.

In the college campus example, you can reduce your own biases by:

- Revisiting the campus on multiple days.

- Meeting students on different parts of the campus, at different times.

- Ensuring you are using the same approach when speaking to all of them.

If you continue to see the same red/extroverted–blue/introverted trend, you can be more and more confident in the accuracy of your predictions. As you continue to gather more information, you may even find other trends that help you predict extraversion even more. For example, you may notice that students who walk in groups are generally more extraverted than students who walk by themselves. With every new (unbiased) trend, you refine your mental model for future decisions.

To improve accuracy over time, Personality AI does the same thing, except with many more data points. Crystal, for example, provides a free personality assessment for all users (thousands each month) and uses the responses to continuously train its own machine learning engine. With every user who completes an assessment, the algorithms can predict personalities with higher accuracy.

HOW PERSONALITY AI LEARNS FROM REAL PEOPLE

The most direct way to understand someone's personality is simple observation. Of course, this isn't possible in most cases and necessitates a tool like Personality AI in the first place. But, by unlocking and organizing personality data in one place and making profiles available between coworkers, friends, and connections, we can collect specific observations from real people and real interactions.

Individually, your observation about how someone behaves is only marginally useful, since you're only one person with a very limited perspective. When you combine observations from many people, however, you can build a 360-degree picture of someone's personality.

Crystal uses traditional personality assessments, text analysis, and attribute analysis as a starting place for understanding someone. Real-life observations make every profile richer and contribute to the entire dataset that future profiles draw from.

VALIDATING AND CORRECTING PERSONALITY PROFILES

With online personality profiles, people can view assessment results and provide their own personal feedback to make that specific profile more accurate, and to tell the machine, *"Hey mister robot! You got this wrong. Do better next time."* This feedback can include:

- Overall accuracy ratings ("I believe this personality profile is 80% accurate").

- Trait-specific insights ("Drew is persuasive, assertive, and outgoing").

- Behavior-specific insights ("Brittney is likely to read instructions thoroughly").

- Situation-specific insights ("Greg was very detail-oriented in this email").

The main benefit of this feedback is that you can capture *perceived* behavior from many sources, including the person themselves, their peers, their coworkers, and anyone else they come into contact with. Personality type can be very subjective when you're relying on one person to describe it. When you have multiple people, however, you can get closer and closer to the truth.

Another benefit of constant feedback is that it helps us understand how an individual's personality changes over time, without having them retake any assessments. By going straight to the sources (i.e. the people who are observing how someone behaves), we can ensure better ongoing reliability than any other method.

Chapter Sixteen

USING PERSONALITY AI TO UNDERSTAND ANYONE

Once you understand the Personality Map and the core elements of Personality AI, you can start to put this powerful technology into practice. With a combination of web-based personality assessments and cutting edge tools like Crystal, anyone who communicates regularly at work can incorporate Personality AI into their daily meetings, phone calls, emails, and other interactions.

USE CASES FOR PERSONALITY AI

As someone who communicates for a living, you may quickly notice many use cases for Personality AI in your everyday professional life. From collaborating with coworkers to selling and recruiting, understanding the behavior and motivations of the people you are communicating with can be tremendously valuable.

Working with Others

Each day, you may have hundreds of tiny, unique interactions with the people you work with. As you work together more, you slowly gain a better understanding of how they work, what they appreciate, and what may frustrate them. Personality AI accelerates the pace at which you understand your coworkers' personalities, enabling you to:

- Build trust and rapport with your coworkers.

- Understand the work pace, environment, and intensity that others prefer.

- Learn the strengths and blind spots of your team as a whole.

Sales, Business Development, and Outreach

While learning about your coworkers' personalities can be complex, at least you have plenty of time to do it since you often interact day after day. It's an entirely different ballgame when your role involves reaching out to strangers outside of your organization for sales or business development. Making a good first impression is often the difference between igniting a conversation or being sent to the trash folder. Personality AI helps you succeed with many types of outreach, such as:

- Sending more effective cold emails.

- Preparing for meetings and phone calls with customers who you do not know well.

- Using the most effective approach for negotiation and persuasion.

- Understanding the core motivations of each customer.

Leadership, Management, and Coaching

If you manage others or serve as a coach, one of your top priorities is likely understanding the interpersonal dynamics of your team so you can set each individual up for success. As a manager, you often learn about your team members through trial and error. When someone reacts poorly to a decision you made or an explanation you gave, you may make a mental note to adjust your style in the future. Personality AI helps you quickly and confidently adjust your style to effectively manage the many unique personality types on your team. Leaders typically use Personality AI to:

- Have more productive and efficient meetings.

- Motivate, encourage, and invest in your team with the right approach.

- Deliver feedback in a way that yields the best results.

- Resolve conflicts as diplomatically as possible.

Recruiting and Team-Building

There are few better examples of the need to understand personalities than when sourcing new employees for a team. Each personality archetype may respond very differently to a job post, interview, or leadership style of the hiring manager. Understanding these differences from the onset of the interview process can help you make a successful, long-term hire instead of a costly mistake. Recruiters and hiring managers tend to leverage Personality AI for:

- Reaching out to new candidates for your team.

- Understanding the right questions to ask in an interview.

- Pitching a role or company in the best possible way.

FINDING QUICK, ACCURATE, AND COMPLETE PERSONALITY PROFILES

Since the situations in your professional life vary widely from one another, there is not a cookie-cutter approach to communication (hence the need for this book). Likewise, there is not a cookie-cutter approach to getting the best possible personality profile.

Remember, the goal of Personality AI is to find someone's personality type as accurately as possible from the information that we have available. Different situations afford you different amounts of information and different spans of time.

In the following chapters, we will describe practical ways to use Personality AI in many of these situations. Sometimes, personality assessments will be your best solution. In other cases, personality predictions with tools like the Crystal Chrome Extension will be better suited.

We will walk through specific scenarios that you can take into work and practice on your own.

PART IV

Communicate Better

Using personality insights for every
conversation

Chapter Seventeen

COMMUNICATING WITH IGNORANCE VERSUS EMPATHY

When connections are cheap, data is abundant, and technology is ubiquitous, everyone tends to be a little bit less trusting. It can be a frustrating time to be a professional communicator, especially one who relies on building new long-term relationships with an audience that is exhausted from hearing packaged, inauthentic messages from every angle.

In a distraction-flooded environment like this, the only way to capture a person's attention is by being intensely relevant. If only that were as easy as it sounds . . .

As flawed, self-centered human beings, we tend to make a lot of assumptions about other people that are actually projections of our own inner thoughts and feelings. These assumptions are often incorrect, and so we plod along in ignorance without understanding why we fail to connect. For example, when I meet someone, my natural tendency is to assume that they prefer to communicate in the same way I do. If I want to have some fun and tell a story, I assume that they probably want to hear my story. If I am the type of person who wants to get right to the point, I assume that they probably want to skip the small talk and also get right to the point.

Our biases make us ignorant by default, and this makes us susceptible to the downside of personality differences—miscommunication, misunderstanding, and many missed opportunities. So far, we have covered how these behavior differences can vary widely between people (even when they share a similar background, job, or environment), and how they create unique challenges. If we choose to ignore them, we drastically minimize our chances at getting what we want out of any given conversation, while maximizing the chances of wasting everyone's time.

To succeed in our communication—especially conversations where we do not know the other person well—we need to battle our own ignorance with *empathy*. Here's a review of the Empathy Equation we covered earlier:

(WHAT someone wants from the interaction) + (WHY they want it) + (HOW they want to interact)

If you have those three basic facts down, you can enter any call, meeting, or email conversation with confidence, because you will be miles ahead of your competition in most cases. Most salespeople, recruiters, and marketers just barely think about the "what." The good ones consider the "why" and only the best understand the "how."

The reason most people cannot use these three elements in their outreach is that it's really hard, or impossible to get the answers if you have never met the person you are contacting. However, Personality AI now makes it possible to fill in the Empathy Equation almost instantly, making it a seamless process to run before every conversation.

Chapter Eighteen

ADAPTING TO DIFFERENT PERSONALITY TYPES

Talking to people with our own personality type is usually much easier than talking to people with different types. The less you need to translate, the less room there is for error, and the less energy it takes to understand each other.

However, our jobs and lives often drop us into uncomfortable situations. We interact with different personality types far more often than similar types, which makes each conversation an adventure and more challenging. Empathy is easy when you naturally understand how the other person is wired, but it can be exceptionally difficult when you don't, and it may feel at times like you're both speaking entirely different languages.

In the following chapters, we are going to break down several common scenarios where you may struggle to communicate well if you do not use empathy and adapt to the other person's style. This includes written communication and verbal communication alike, and we will explain how you can apply Personality AI to succeed against steep odds in all of them.

Before we get to the scenarios, it's important to understand some more general advice for interacting with each personality type. Tailoring your communication style does not come naturally and takes practice for most people, but starting with the simplest guidelines, outlined in Table 18.1, can help you develop the right habits.

Table 18.1 General guidelines for communicating with each personality type.

ARCHETYPE	DO	DON'T
D: Architects, Captains, Drivers, Initiators	• Face them directly, with confidence and boldness. • Explain what you want to get out of the meeting. • Speak with some urgency and intensity.	• Act overly reserved or timid. • Take too much time to explain who you are. • Use pleasantries or small talk any more than necessary.
I: Influencers, Motivators, Encouragers, Harmonizers	• Communicate with high energy and enthusiasm. • Stay lighthearted and playful. • Find ways to connect personally and provide genuine compliments.	• Start the conversation with any criticism or negativity. • Be overly skeptical. • Explain lots of details right away.

Table 18.1 (continued)

ARCHETYPE	DO	DON'T
S: Counselors, Supporters, Planners, Stabilizers	• Express gratitude for their time and anything they have done so far. • Take some time to explain your background. • Communicate with warmth and sincerity.	• Get to your main point too abruptly. • Move the conversation at a rapid pace. • Be overly intense.
C: Editors, Analysts, Skeptics, Questioners	• Display a calm, collected demeanor and control over your emotions. • Speak with specific, descriptive language. • Ask factual, intellectually stimulating questions.	• Ask questions that are too probing or personal. • Use embellishments or vague language. • Be overly emotional.

Chapter Nineteen

PERSONALITY AI FOR EMAIL OUTREACH

Professionals in sales, business development, recruiting, and other outreach-oriented roles have always been fighting an uphill battle for their prospects' attention, and technology has thrown a monkey wrench into the mix. As sales and marketing automation tools have proliferated and promised more efficiency, they have had the infuriating side effect of flooding buyers' inboxes with messages that sound more and more similar.

Kyle Porter, the CEO of SalesLoft, highlights this problem in a piece he wrote for *Forbes*:[1]

> A mediocre sales organization is one that doesn't understand that an SDR is a crucial entry point to your company for a potential prospect. They're prioritizing output over results, feelings over data and doing as little thought as possible, ultimately treating a role that is incredibly important as interchangeable.

According to the research organization TOPO, it takes an average sales representative 18 calls to connect with one buyer, and four emails to get one recipient to even open one of them.[2]

---

[1] Forbes Council, "Bad Sales Development Is Killing Sales—and Here's How We Can Stop It," https://www.forbes.com/sites/forbesbusinessdevelopmentcouncil/2017/08/11/bad-sales-development-is-killing-sales-and-heres-how-we-can-stop-it/#6ca5f33a6997.
[2] "Sales Development Technology: The Stack Emerges," https://blog.topohq.com/sales-development-technology-the-stack-emerges/.

I personally get inundated with dozens of requests every day, so I can only imagine the chaos that takes place in a larger company executive's inbox.

"Can we schedule 30 minutes this week . . ."

"Can you tell me who the right person to speak with on your team about . . ."

"Bumping this up to the top of your inbox in case you missed it!" (That's my favorite.)

Porter insists that this boilerplate, quantity-over-quality approach to sales development is killing the industry as a whole. Instead, he recommends a more empathetic approach with "human communication."

> Human communication sounds and reads like you're having a conversation that feels real rather than a forced, uncaring sales pitch. Nobody picks this up overnight, but it's something that can be learned . . . You also have to give [your team] the tools to execute personalization at scale so that they can realistically reach their targets without removing their humanity.

While the majority of outreach professionals rely on their tools to send out mass, standardized emails, this cloud of spam creates opportunity for senders who have a more thoughtful approach. A study by Drift and Outreach found that personalized email messages had an almost 50% higher response rate than standard, automated messages.[3] Furthermore, those personalized emails were more than twice as effective when they were sent to lists of under 100 people.

Email is still the most important medium for businesses to reach new customers, but outreach emails only seem to be getting more difficult. This is a perfect place to start applying Personality AI.

[3] Adam Schoenfeld, "What 290 Cold Emails Teach Us About Sales & Marketing in 2019," Drift, https://www.drift.com/blog/cold-email-study/#cold-emails-deck.

PREPARING THE EMAIL

Unlike the sales reps and recruiters of a few decades ago, who had little more than a name and a phone number, you likely have access to far more data about your prospects before you ever speak with them. Personality AI can use this abundance of data to accurately predict someone's personality type before you meet them, and provide on-demand advice for communicating effectively.

Crystal mainly does this with its Chrome extension (extensions are apps that can plug into a web browser and be used as you browse different websites). When you view someone's LinkedIn profile, for example, the Crystal Chrome extension analyzes the text on the profile and provides a personality prediction along with specific communication advice (see Figure 19.1).

Once you have a personality profile, you can start preparing for your conversation.

WHAT DO THEY WANT?

For this first variable of the Empathy Equation, it may seem that the answer is totally dependent on your product or service. However, if you peel away one or two layers, you'll realize that you're not selling what you think you're selling.

People with different personality types are usually looking for vastly different things at the deepest level, even from the same product. For example, an *Analyst (C)* may buy a Tesla Model 3 because it is the most fuel efficient, high-performing vehicle on the market. A *Motivator (I)*, on the other hand, may purchase that same exact car because it's fun to drive and gets lots of attention in a crowd.

Tesla is selling one product, but the customers are buying *two* different benefits. In fact, every type tends to look for different benefits (see Table 19.1), and sometimes they are conflicting.

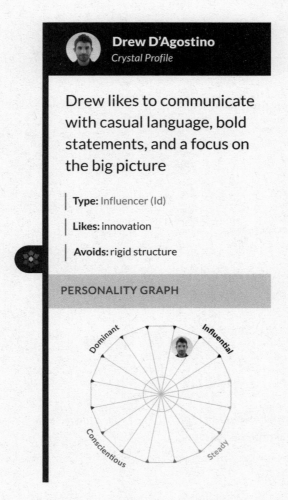

Figure 19.1 The Crystal Chrome Extension predicting a personality.

Once you know *what* you're actually selling, you can move on to the next step . . .

WHY DO THEY WANT IT?

Core motivations are difficult to assess, and your own motivations may not even be entirely clear to you. Still, Personality AI can help us take a very good guess at what may be driving our prospect's actions.

Table 19.1 Benefits that attract each personality type.

TYPE	PREFERRED BENEFITS
D: Architects, Captains, Drivers, Initiators	• Immediate results. • Competitive advantage. • Impact on bottom line.
I: Influencers, Motivators, Encouragers, Harmonizers	• New relationships. • Fun experiences. • Novelty.
S: Counselors, Supporters, Planners, Stabilizers	• Security. • Dependability. • Long-term trust.
C: Editors, Analysts, Skeptics, Questioners	• Accuracy. • High quality. • Efficiency.

Even though you may be preparing for a short, one-time conversation, it's important to consider that you are only meeting someone in a snapshot of their life. To you, they are a *dot*. But to themselves, they are a *line* with past experiences and future dreams. Core motivations are affected by both.

If you can understand someone's personality archetype, as well as any other background information on what they have done in the past or what they are aiming for in the future, you can try to infer some basic motivations. Table 19.2 shows a few general guidelines based on the Personality Map.

Table 19.2 Core motivations for each personality type.

ARCHETYPE	CORE MOTIVATIONS
D: Architects, Captains, Drivers, Initiators	• Rapid advancement. • Growing authority. • More control over the future.
I: Influencers, Motivators, Encouragers, Harmonizers	• Excitement for the future. • Feeling of being unique. • Peer recognition.
S: Counselors, Supporters, Planners, Stabilizers	• A predictable future. • Less chance of conflict. • Well-being of people around them.
C: Editors, Analysts, Skeptics, Questioners	• Expanding knowledge and skills. • Minimizing unknowns. • Logical plans for the future.

Be careful not to overanalyze or overstate someone's motivations, because it's easy to misfire and sabotage your outreach.
However, if you can do some investigative work before the first conversation and continue to ask questions throughout the relationship, understanding core motivations can be the most powerful part of the Empathy Equation for building strong and lasting trust.

HOW DO THEY WANT TO INTERACT?

The *what* and *why* largely dictate the substance of your outreach message, but the *how* gives you the style.

Every archetype has a preferred communication style, as shown in Table 19.3.

Tailoring your communication style is a skill you can acquire over time. As you start doing outreach with personality types in mind, you will notice trends. *D*-types tend to write things in one way and use certain phrases, while *S*-types use other phrases. It all comes with practice.

Table 19.3 Communication style of each personality type.

ARCHETYPE	COMMUNICATION STYLE
D: Architects, Captains, Drivers, Initiators	• Direct. • Brief. • Business-like.
I: Influencers, Motivators, Encouragers, Harmonizers	• Casual. • Expressive. • Colorful.
S: Counselors, Supporters, Planners, Stabilizers	• Friendly. • Warm. • Polite.
C: Editors, Analysts, Skeptics, Questioners	• Formal. • Literal. • Descriptive.

WRITING THE EMAIL

The best way to learn how to use an empathy-driven approach in outreach is by example. In this section, we will go through some common situations that you can use as a guide for your own emails.

Email to Schedule a Meeting

In any role involving outreach, you're likely to send lots of emails with a simple purpose—*get the other person to talk to me*.

> **SUBJECT: Preferred IT vendors | [COMPANY]**
>
> Hi Drew,
>
> Happy to connect whenever time permits for a quick introduction to see how we can assist you with your development needs.
>
> I am with a [PLACE] based Software services and Analytics company, [COMPANY] Inc. with corporate office in [PLACE] and Offshore development centers in [PLACE]. We have delivered solutions in the space of Custom Development (Web & Mobile), Business Intelligence, Data Analytics, Visualization, Artificial Intelligence, Machine Learning, Blockchain, and Chatbots to our clients across the USA and Europe.
>
> Based on your availability, I'd love to set up a telecon to take you through our corporate overview, share our experience working with companies like yours, their challenges, and our solutions. I would also like to understand your pain points/challenges/road map for this year and how we can add value to your business.
>
> Does it make sense for us to talk? If so, kindly let me know your availability for a quick chat.
>
> Thanks & Regards,
> [OMITTED] | Regional Head – Business Development

As a company leader with a pulse, I get many, many of these emails. My inbox is inundated, actually, so it wasn't hard to find one that we can tear apart, such as the example on the previous page.

It seems like a perfectly reasonable message, right?

In the grammatical sense, sure. It was a safe message, one that nobody is getting fired for. But was it effective? Certainly not.

Let's look at this through the lens of the Empathy Equation.

What Do I Want?

This friendly sales rep is trying to sell me software and analytics services, which I am well-qualified for as the CEO of a technology company. As an *Influencer (Id)* toward the top of the Personality Map, I would be looking for these kinds of benefits from a vendor:

- A more creative, innovative approach.

- Speed and flexibility.

- Common connections and interests.

Instead of that, the sales rep gave me:

- A huge list of every type of project they do.

- A broad request to understand my "pain points" and "road map."

- A general reference to their past experience and credibility.

Why Do I Want It?

Influencers and other similar archetypes have motivations that sometimes seem irrational to others. These include:

- Recognition and praise from our peers.

- Desire to be unique, even at a high cost.

- High upside in the future, even at a high risk.

Instead, the sales rep tried appealing to very different motivations that were simply not compelling to an *Influencer (Id)*, like:

- Predictability, based on social proof: When I read "share experiences working with companies like mine," someone with my personality type thinks, "We're going to get a cookie-cutter solution."

- Security, based on size: By mentioning all of their locations, he was trying to make the company sound big, but I perceived that as potentially bureaucratic, slow-moving, and risk-averse.

How Do I Want to Communicate?

Even if the sales rep had written better content, directly addressing the major desires and motivations of an *Influencer (Id)*, it would have been spoiled by the fact that I didn't actually read most of this email.

Style can be even more important than substance sometimes, and here's where he got it wrong:

- *Influencers* prefer short, high-level emails. This one was four paragraphs long and filled with unessential detail.

- *Influencers* prefer casual, personable language. This one was written with a very formal tone. Though polite, it did not create the kind of connection that drives me to action.

- *Influencers* are persuaded by direct, black-and-white calls to action. We need to be "pinned down," otherwise we move onto the next thing. Instead of saying something like "Can I send over a proposal?," this email used hesitant, overly cautious phrases like "Happy to connect whenever time permits . . ." and "Let me know your availability for a quick chat . . ."

This wasn't a *bad* email necessarily. It may have been effective for a *C*-type (*Analyst, Editor, Skeptic, Questioner*) personality, or even an *S*-type (*Counselor, Supporter, Planner, Stabilizer*), but certainly not for an *Influencer (Id)* like me.

If I were to rewrite this email in a way that gets my attention and drives me to action, it would look something like this...

SUBJECT: We can help you innovate faster

Hey Drew,

We are a Houston-based software company that helps fast-growing startups move faster, without putting in all of the mundane work and high cost that comes with hiring a larger team internally.

It seems like we both have expertise in Artificial Intelligence and Machine Learning. I would love to show you some of the more innovative projects we have produced recently.

Do you have any upcoming projects that you would consider outsourcing? If so, I would like to send a proposal.

Thanks,
Harry
Regional Head – Business Development

Beauty is in the eye of the beholder, and emails are judged by the impact on the recipient.

SENDING FOLLOW-UP EMAILS

Even if your email is written in the right style to appeal to the recipient's personality, there's no guarantee you'll get an answer on the first try. To the contrary, 80% of sales happen after at least five follow-ups.[4] This means that follow-up emails are incredibly important in order to make your outreach successful.

Not surprisingly, the ideal format of a follow-up email varies greatly based on the personality type of the recipient. Consider this follow-up email my colleague Jonathan recently received:

SUBJECT: Following Up

Hi Jonathan,

I hope you enjoyed the holidays! Did you do anything fun for New Years?

I wanted to follow up on the email I sent last month. If it makes sense, it would be great to reconnect for a brief update call and to see if [COMPANY] can be helpful now or at some point down the road.

Please let me know if you have any availability over the next couple of weeks.

Best,
[NAME]

[4] Study by MarketingDonut, https://www.marketingdonut.co.uk/sales/sales-techniques-and-negotiations/why-you-must-follow-up-leads.

This is another perfectly reasonable, polite email. However, to someone with an *Analyst (C)* personality type like Jonathan, this message will never earn a reply. In fact, it will just about ensure that Jonathan will have no interest in connecting with this sales rep.

As an *Analyst (C)* toward the bottom left of the Personality Map, Jonathan is likely to appreciate a follow-up email that:

- Is written with formal, business-like language.

- Includes a recap of the details previously discussed.

- Is specific with a literal ask.

Unfortunately, this email missed the mark in several areas:

- *Analysts* build trust slowly as they get to know someone, and initially can be skeptical. Asking a personal question about Jonathan's New Year's plans can come across as a violation of his personal space.

- *Analysts* appreciate detail and specifics. They tend to do a lot of research before making a decision. Not including any additional facts in the follow-up is a quick way to lose Jonathan's attention.

- *Analysts* are literal when they speak. If you ask an *Analyst* a vague question that doesn't have a black or white response, don't expect a great answer. Jonathan is unlikely to respond well to sharing his availability over the next several weeks.

If I want to earn Jonathan's attention, I might rewrite the email like this:

> **SUBJECT: [COMPANY] — Software Consulting — Follow-Up**
>
> Hello Jonathan,
>
> I'm following up on the email I sent in mid-December regarding IT services for Crystal. As a brief reminder:
>
> - We are a global IT services firm with 12 locations throughout the United States, Canada, and Europe.
> - We have been Amazon Web Services and Microsoft Azure certified partners for 7 years.
> - We've completed 19 projects for organizations similar to Crystal over the last year.
>
> I understand you are maintaining a complex technical architecture at Crystal. Are there areas that my IT team could assist?
>
> If so, would Tuesday at 9am EST or Wednesday at 3pm EST work for a 30-minute call to discuss further?
>
> Best Regards,
> [NAME]

While this highly specific email would likely be ineffective for me as an *Influencer (Id)*, it is an ideal structure to communicate with an *Analyst (C)* like Jonathan.

THE FOUR PRIMARY EMAIL STYLES

While this example contained two email styles, each personality type has specific email preferences (see Table 19.4). These include variations in the content, language, and tone of each component of the message, like the greeting, subject line, body, and call to action.

Table 19.4 Email preferences.

ARCHETYPE	DO	DON'T
D: Architects, Captains, Drivers, Initiators	• Keep the subject and body very short. • Include a clear, direct call-to-action that they can complete immediately. • Use business-like language.	• Include too much detail. • Ask lots of open-ended questions. • Send unnecessary attachments or links. • Use overly expressive or verbose language.
I: Influencers, Motivators, Encouragers, Harmonizers	• Include images and media where possible. • Write with a positive, upbeat tone. • Use casual, colorful language.	• Write with an overly formal or serious tone. • Include lots of raw data without explaining the important insights. • Use forceful or high-pressure language.

Table 19.4 (continued)

ARCHETYPE	DO	DON'T
S: Counselors, Supporters, Planners, Stabilizers	• Include a warm, personal greeting and sincere sign-off. • Refer to common relationships, interests, and associations. • Use friendly, expressive language.	• Include an overly direct or binary call-to-action. • Write in a concise way that could be perceived as cold. • Drift too far away from email standards and conventions that they are used to.
C: Editors, Analysts, Skeptics, Questioners	• Include lots of detail and descriptions. • Ask clear questions and ask for the reasons behind their responses. • Use formal, serious language.	• Use casual language. • Leave out any important details. • Write with an emotionally expressive tone.

Chapter Twenty

PERSONALITY AI FOR SALES MEETINGS

You can spend hours crafting the perfect email, but when you're in the middle of a sales meeting or on a call, you don't have that luxury. The conversation is real-time, so the entire trust-building process is accelerated.

This makes preparation even more important, since you will need to think on your feet and quickly adjust your approach as the conversation evolves. When you're having a high-impact business negotiation, you are very likely to be swayed by emotions, as well.

EXAMPLE OF A SALES CONVERSATION IMPROVED BY PERSONALITY AI

Let's say you have a meeting planned with Greg for this very purpose. You're a commercial real estate agent trying to get him to sign a new lease on office space downtown, and while you are close to agreement, there are still some important terms to work out.

Without any awareness of Greg's personality, here are some examples of what you might say in this sales situation:

- "I'm glad you like the space. I think your employees will love it, too."

- "Think about the possibilities for the lobby area. We can design that room to look amazing."

- "My other clients have been asking about this building for a long time."

- "The location is very convenient. You can walk right down the street to a bunch of bars and restaurants."

- "The natural light and hardwood floors are the best part."

I specifically wrote those phrases because they would come naturally to my personality, as an *Influencer (Id)* on the top right of the Personality Map. I'm always trying to tell a good story and appeal to emotions, and I tend to focus on features that are particularly visual or social. However, that style may not be very effective in a sales meeting with someone like Greg. If you are similar to me (or otherwise different from Greg), you will need to adjust your approach.

Greg is an *Architect (Dc)*, which means he is a pragmatic, results-driven executor who can sniff out inefficiencies and change his mind quickly based on new information. For this call, you will need to do your homework if you want him to sign on the dotted line.

Here's what an empathy-driven approach would look like . . .

What

In an office lease, Greg is probably looking for:

- Competitive pricing compared to the rest of the local market.

- Detailed cost breakdowns and information about additional costs that he may need to account for in the future.

- Clear rules and terms, without any vague legal language that could create a disadvantage.

Why

As an *Architect (Dc)*, Greg is primarily driven by motivations like:

- Winning the best possible deal for his company to reduce costs.

- Having as much clarity and visibility into the future as possible.

- Understanding the underlying intentions and trustworthiness of the other parties involved.

How

When negotiating, *Architects* like Greg tend to:

- Maintain tight control over information.

- Use firm or forceful language to push for a better outcome.

- Ask lots of questions to understand the motivations of the other side.

- Criticize any potential inaccuracies or inflated claims.

Rather than the more emotional and socially focused approach I demonstrated before, you could be more effective by applying the Empathy Equation to this meeting from the start:

- "Based on the current market rates in this area, you will be paying slightly below average for a very high-quality space."

- "The location has lots of parking available and is very close to mass transit, so employees can be efficient with their time."

- "Everything is fairly turnkey, so there will be minimal cost to getting it ready for move-in."

- "There is room to grow beyond your team size now, but you are allowed to sublease the extra space in the meantime."

- "I can give you a sheet with all of the important terms of the lease."

This is an entirely different conversation, and it would likely be much more effective with an *Architect (Dc)* like Greg.

Architects and other *D*-types may seem difficult to negotiate with, but that's only true if you aren't prepared. If you enter the discussion with big ideas but no data to back them up, the process will indeed be grueling and exhausting for both parties. People on the left side of the map do not often shy away from confrontation, and people on the top half tend to dig in their heels. The *D*-types are in the top left, so you may encounter both.

However, as someone who negotiates regularly with *Architects* and other personalities on the left side of the Personality Map, I can tell you that it's actually quite refreshing once you learn how to assemble your thoughts in a clear, action-oriented way. *Architects* can be fast, rational, and bold with their decisions once they have all the facts. You'll never need to guess what they are thinking, and they usually will not change their mind based on a gut feeling.

ADAPTING AND REACTING AS THE CONVERSATION PROGRESSES

These examples have largely focused on the preparation and early stages of a conversation. However, once the conversation starts, the rubber meets the road and your theory becomes reality.

Personality AI makes it easy to prepare for any of these scenarios. A tool like Crystal can give you a full cheat sheet for a meeting based on the specific person, the medium, and the goal of the meeting. In addition, you have all the time you need to learn more information beyond personality to help guide your approach. All of this makes you more confident.

During the meeting, however, you cannot lean as heavily on the technology. You may need to adjust your style based on the other person's mood, ask more questions to understand their goals better, or any other number of pivots. Improvising is a skill that does not come naturally to most people, but in this case, the Personality Map can help us shoot from the hip a little bit less and have a real framework for fast-moving conversation.

Changing Your Style

Sometimes, you may incorrectly assess a person's archetype before meeting them. Your Personality AI application might even predict it wrong. They might simply be in a weird mood on that day, or they may be adapting their personality to a new role.

Whatever the reason, people sometimes behave differently than you think they will, especially in a first meeting. When this happens, you need to adjust your style in a hurry.

You will not always have the data or technology on hand to find someone's profile with Personality AI, so it's important to understand the basics of how each archetype prefers to communicate in a call or meeting; see Tables 20.1 and 20.2.

Table 20.1 Phone call preferences.

ARCHETYPE	DO	DON'T
D: Architects, Captains, Drivers, Initiators	• Ask for a window of time to call, rather than wait for a specific scheduled appointment. • Get right into the main point for your call. • Explicitly state your goals before you begin the discussion.	• Use lots of time for small talk before getting to the point. • Speak with a reserved or passive tone. • Allow them to move the pace of the call faster than you are comfortable with.
I: Influencers, Motivators, Encouragers, Harmonizers	• Ask if they are available for an immediate call (via text, email, or direct message), rather than plan in advance. • Suggest a video call instead of voice. • Begin the call with small talk to build rapport.	• Speak with a tone that is too serious or formal. • Get into lots of details unless they specifically ask. • React in a cold or distant way to their emotional appeals.

(continued)

Table 20.1 (continued)

ARCHETYPE	DO	DON'T
S: Counselors, Supporters, Planners, Stabilizers	• Ask questions about their feelings and motivations before asking them to take action. • Express appreciation for their time and attention. • Use a friendly, warm approach.	• Push the discussion forward too quickly. • Use blunt or terse language to make your point. • Ask for an immediate action or decision on the phone.
C: Editors, Analysts, Skeptics, Questioners	• Communicate the most important details in writing before speaking on the phone. • Provide links, data, and other references before or during the call. • Use serious, unemotional language.	• Suggest a video call without specific reasons. • Interrupt them or change subjects. • Reach a conclusion quickly, before explaining your reasons.

Table 20.2 Meeting preferences.

ARCHETYPE	DO	DON'T
D: Architects, Captains, Drivers, Initiators	• Make your main points and goals clear in the first few minutes. • Ask direct yes-or-no questions. • Ask them to set the meeting location and environment.	• Require too much preparation or reading before the meeting. • Let the meeting last any longer than it needs to be. • Bring others into the meeting unless it is necessary.
I: Influencers, Motivators, Encouragers, Harmonizers	• Incorporate food or drinks into the meeting. • Use visual aids wherever possible. • Be animated and emphatic.	• Have the meeting in an isolated, closed space. • Present lots of resources or anything else that could be a distraction. • Get agitated if they are slightly late.

(continued)

Table 20.2 *(continued)*

ARCHETYPE	DO	DON'T
S: Counselors, Supporters, Planners, Stabilizers	• Meet in a relaxed, peaceful environment. • Set expectations up front for the length and content of the discussion. • Take time to catch up before getting into business discussions.	• Apply pressure to make a decision on the spot. • Wait for them to set a meeting location and time. • Take over the conversation without asking them more questions.
C: Editors, Analysts, Skeptics, Questioners	• Provide plenty of information beforehand. • Include as few people as you can. • Allow them sufficient personal space.	• Have the meeting in a public space around lots of other people. • Ask lots of personal questions before earning their trust. • Make bold claims without logic or data to back them up.

DRIVING SOMEONE TO TAKE ACTION

For professional communicators, most daily conversations have a specific end goal in mind. Therefore, after learning about the other person's needs and understanding what they are trying to accomplish, the purpose of the conversation becomes *driving someone to take an action*.

This can encompass many goals, like convincing someone to:

- Leave their job and join your company.

- Buy your product instead of your competitors' product.

- Sign a contract to do business with you.

- Accept an invitation for your event.

- Donate money to a cause.

- Increase your salary.

These are often some of the toughest conversations you will need to have in your career, so it is critical to speak and write persuasively.

We may think of "persuasion" as a dirty word. I think of the car salesman Jerry Lundegaard from the movie *Fargo*, relentlessly insisting on the "TruCoat" finish and cornering his customers into paying more than they already agreed upon. Indeed, there is a slimy kind of persuasion.

In *Influence: The Psychology of Persuasion*, Dr. Robert Cialdini outlines six principles of influence—persuasive tactics that people and organizations have successfully used to induce action for as long as we have been able to speak. These principles—*Reciprocity, Consistency, Social Proof, Authority, Liking,* and *Scarcity*—are neutral tools. Cialdini's book describes them in detail, so you can both use them to accomplish your own benevolent goals and recognize when someone else is using them for a less benevolent one.

As our economy has become more connected, transparent, and relationship-oriented, it is much harder to use the persuasion tactics in a malicious way. People simply have too many options. And there are too many ways to sniff out a bad actor.

Instead, professional communicators should see persuasion as a long-term strategy. We want to understand the needs of our audience and guide them through a decision-making process. Of course, we're looking to drive a specific outcome. But our role in that process is more to *help the person convince themselves to take action*, rather than to induce their action through force or coercion.

Blaise Pascal described this approach more than 350 years ago:

> People are generally better persuaded by the reasons which they have themselves discovered than by those which have come into the mind of others.[1]

In a world with unlimited supply, this is more of a rule than a suggestion. So, how do we coach our prospects, customers, and colleagues through their own decision-making process in a way that builds long-term trust? Consult Table 20.3.

---

[1] Olivia Goldhill, "A philosopher's 350-year-old trick to get people to change their minds is now backed up by psychologists," *Quartz*, September 11, 2016, https://qz.com/778767/to-tell-someone-theyre-wrong-first-tell-them-how-theyre-right/.

Table 20.3 How to effectively persuade each type.

ARCHETYPE	DO	DON'T
D: Architects, Captains, Drivers, Initiators	• Provide a high-level summary of value. • React quickly to their feedback. • Use an energetic, assertive tone. • Focus on competitive advantages.	• Go into too much detail. • Use a hesitant, passive tone. • Take a long time to get to the core value. • Bounce around between multiple points.
I: Influencers, Motivators, Encouragers, Harmonizers	• Talk about the other people who have taken the action you want them to take. • Use expressive, colorful language. • Send visual aids via email or screenshare. • Try to keep the conversation focused.	• Use an overly serious tone. • Leave next steps ambiguous. • Use overly descriptive language. • Talk too much about past experience.

(continued)

Table 20.3 (continued)

ARCHETYPE	DO	DON'T
S: Counselors, Supporters, Planners, Stabilizers	• Walk them through the buying process. • Tell them about your credentials and experience. • Ask about their concerns and risks. • Use a warm, friendly tone.	• Ask probing questions before you have built rapport. • Focus on results without considering people-related factors. • Use a demanding or pushy tone. • Downplay their current way of doing things.
C: Editors, Analysts, Skeptics, Questioners	• Use a serious, business-like tone. • Bring up your flaws before they do. • Ask about their toughest problems. • Send additional data to support your pitch.	• Try to engage in too much small talk. • Be unrealistically optimistic. • Use emotional, colorful language. • Skip over details.

HANDLING OBJECTIONS

In a conversation where your goal is to drive action, the hardest part is often managing the unforeseen obstacles that pop up. When a prospect or customer voices an *objection* that you have not prepared for, it can be jarring. It can also sound like a dead end.

However, an objection may also be an indicator that you're onto something. Objections are a form of micro-conflict. Conflict is uncomfortable for most people. So, most people do not introduce conflict into a discussion unless they really care about something. The objection that sounds like a deal-breaker on the surface might be a clue that the person is doing the diligent work of checking off boxes and accounting for all the risks before making a final decision. You may be helping them clear their last few mental hurdles.

Since we are talking about the later stages of a conversation here, specific objections are heavily dependent on the situation and it is difficult to make any blanket predictions based on personality. Still, different personality archetypes have varying sensitivities and risk tolerances, so understanding their pre-decision thought patterns can help you anticipate the nature of the objections they may bring up, if not the questions themselves (see Table 20.4).

Table 20.4 Likely objections and concerns before making a decision.

ARCHETYPE	EXAMPLE CONCERN
D: Architects, Captains, Drivers, Initiators	• This might not happen as fast as I want it to. • This decision might be more costly than I expect. • I may be able to find a better option somewhere else.

(continued)

233

Table 20.4 (*continued*)

ARCHETYPE	EXAMPLE CONCERN
I: Influencers, Motivators, Encouragers, Harmonizers	• Something better may come along after I have committed to this decision. • This decision might not have enough upside if things go really well. • I may lose the ability to be flexible or creative.
S: Counselors, Supporters, Planners, Stabilizers	• Things may change in the future. • I may trust you but need to work with different people whom I do not trust. • This decision could be more risky than I am comfortable with.
C: Editors, Analysts, Skeptics, Questioners	• The data backing up your claims may not be accurate. • You might be leaving out important details. • I may be able to do it better myself.

Chapter Twenty-One

PERSONALITY AI FOR DIFFICULT CONVERSATIONS

Empathy can make your outreach and sales conversations more productive, but it can likely make an even bigger impact on your most important (and most difficult) conversations. Even when you have known and worked with someone for a long time, stressful or unpredictable situations can force people to retreat into their base-level impulses and double down on their natural behavior patterns.

Personality profiles can give us really important insights about how someone is thinking when it matters most. In this chapter, we will cover some specific examples of common high-stakes situations that you may face in your career, and how to approach them with personality data.

SCENARIO: ASKING FOR A RAISE

For most people, one of the most difficult and anxiety-inducing conversations of their career can be asking their boss for a raise. It's an intimidating task, and a delicate subject. But in our economy, there aren't many better ways to directly and immediately impact your financial life.

Still, you can approach a meeting like this with the Empathy Equation and walk into the room with confidence. The preparation is very similar to our previous examples.

This time, let's say you're a designer working for an advertising agency. You are preparing to meet with your boss, Brittney, on your two-year anniversary of working at the firm, ready to ask for an ambitious, but reasonable 7% pay raise.

If you were getting general advice for this meeting, here's what someone might tell you to say:

- "I have created lots of value in the past year and I should be compensated accordingly."

- "I love my job here, but if I am unable to earn what I am worth, then I will need to look at other options."

- "According to this market data, I should be making $X per year."

- "I want to do whatever I can to advance and achieve my goals."

- "If possible, I would like to settle this by the end of the week."

All of it could be good advice for someone who is more direct in these kinds of conversations, especially if they appreciate external data and debating the merits of certain claims. However, Brittney is a *Planner (Sc)*, in the lower bottom right region of the Personality Map. This type of person requires a less direct, more patient, more relational approach.

Knowing this, here is how you could approach the meeting . . .

What

Assuming the nature of your work isn't changing too much, Brittney probably wants:

- Close, mutually trusting relationships with the members of her team.

- Steady, consistent results that she can confidently predict.

- A long-term commitment from you, to continue producing at a high level and for you to help coach and develop other employees.

Why

As a *Planner (Sc)*, Brittney tends to be motivated by:

- Having a higher employee retention rate than other leaders in the company.

- Creating a peaceful, welcoming environment for herself and her team.

- Helping her colleagues feel supported, heard, and appreciated.

How

Luckily, *Planners* tend to be among the easier archetypes to talk to because they are such good listeners. When you meet with Brittney, you should:

- Use an approachable, personable, and warm demeanor.

- Take time to catch up with small talk before getting into your main request.

- Ask how she wants to develop the team in the future as it grows.

Armed with the Empathy Equation, you would enter the meeting with confidence, but with a much gentler attitude. Here are some phrases you could keep in your back pocket:

- "I sincerely value the commitment that you have shown to my development and personal growth."

- "I want to be in this for the long haul and give you security that I am not going anywhere."

- "How have you looked at pay increases in the past, and what could I do to make you feel comfortable with it?"

- "For the future, I would like to take more informal responsibility for coaching and supporting new members of the team."

- "You can let me know what you decide after you have had some time to think about it."

Unlike *Architects* or *Influencers*, *Planners* generally do not make decisions quickly. They may need to let things sit and marinate for a while before coming to a conclusion, so at the end of your meeting with Brittney it may be unwise to apply pressure for a decision on the spot. Instead, you should respectfully but consistently follow up about your request in the coming days.

SCENARIO: GIVING FEEDBACK

Providing constructive feedback can be a delicate balancing act. On one hand, you don't want to come across as too harsh and offend the person. At the same time, if you provide feedback that is too soft and beat around the bush, the other person may never improve. There is a balance to strike, and that balance is different for each personality.

Suppose you are giving a website designer feedback on a new web page he created. For someone with a warmer, more outgoing personality like an *Encourager (Is)*, *Harmonizer (IS)*, or *Counselor (Si)*, you might use a gentle, polite approach to deliver feedback. For example:

- Wrap your criticisms with positivity and more emotional language.

- Brainstorm and discuss creative approaches to make it better.

- Bring up new ideas.

- Get more people involved in providing feedback.

These examples may be what you'd imagine as the default way to provide polite feedback. However, what if you are giving feedback to James, who is a *Questioner (CD)*? In that case, the conversations need to be much more direct, calculated, and methodical. You might approach the meeting like this:

What

As a *Questioner (CD)*, James probably wants to:

- Eliminate the flaws in his own thinking.

- Achieve the best result he is capable of in the shortest period of time.

- Quickly process feedback so he can get back to work.

Why

As a *Questioner (CD)*, James tends to be motivated by:

- Advancing quickly and proving himself.

- Creating an end-result that is high quality and works correctly.

- Autonomy to solve complex problems independently.

How

For better or worse, *Questioners* may be a bit more challenging to provide with feedback. This is because they are confident, accurate, and rely on heavy research to change their minds. When meeting with James, you may want to:

- Be direct and forceful when making your point, so your convictions are clear. He likely prefers the harsh reality, rather than any ambiguity about how he can improve.

- Present your feedback as facts, ideally backed up by research or data, rather than opinions that are influenced by emotion.

- Be prepared for pushback if James disagrees with your feedback. Do not worry about softening up the language, since James doesn't mind conflict in order to get to the best result.

The Empathy Equation enables you to walk into a meeting with James prepared to be productive. Here are some phrases that might particularly resonate with a *Questioner (CD)*:

- "I'm going to challenge you on this part . . ."
- "Thinking back to the goal we started with . . ."
- "Compared to the other solutions I have seen . . ."
- "I have a few specific ways for you to improve . . ."

Expect that your feedback session with James will likely be productive and brief. *Questioners* like him often work quickly to implement any feedback you clearly agreed to in the meeting.

SCENARIO: RESOLVING CONFLICT

In the professional world, conflict is inevitable. Our differences in personality, opinions, visions, and goals can sometimes create misalignment. In order to be productive, that conflict needs to be resolved. However, poorly handled conflict can be destructive: it can get personal and people can get hurt unnecessarily.

When it comes to conflict, we don't want to merely minimize the damage. We can use healthy conflict as a way to learn about each other, build deeper, more genuine relationships, and achieve superior results. The Personality Map can help us navigate our most contentious, emotionally charged situations with empathy, tact, and clarity. With a little preparation, you can be more thoughtful about approaching conflict and meet the other person where they are.

Consider, again, James, the *Questioner (CD)*. This time, James is working with Austin, a *Motivator (I)*, and they have a misunderstanding about deadlines. They are working on a client project and James wants to push for a short deadline so they work efficiently. However, Austin wants a longer deadline to leave space for creativity, innovation, and exploring new ideas. It's unclear what the *right* answer is, but it is clear that they are misaligned, and they need to sort through this situation before it becomes a more significant conflict.

If James was acting in his natural *Questioner (CD)* style, without adjusting, he would likely:

- Use very accurate, blunt language to describe why his position is correct. This might sound overly harsh to Austin and cause him to be defensive.

- Try to gain as much control over time, process, and the other logistical aspects of the decision as possible. This could make Austin feel constrained.

- Seek resolution with focused, emotionally detached debate. Austin will likely incorporate emotions regardless. This imbalance can make the debates feel like personal affronts rather than objective reasoning.

By using the Empathy Equation, James can adjust his style to better collaborate with Austin.

What

Austin is most likely focused on having:

- A friendly, positive relationship regardless of the outcome from this particular dispute.

- Freedom to devise and try new solutions.

Why

Consider what is most important to Austin as a *Motivator (I)*:

- Austin thrives off of positive energy, both internally and from the people around him.

- Austin likes to pursue curiosity and innovation.

How

By understanding the *What* and *Why*, James can adjust his style to effectively resolve conflict with Austin by:

- Providing verbal reassurance that they are on the same team and that this debate does not imply any lack of trust or liking for Austin.

- Allowing Austin to brainstorm new solutions without quickly shooting them down.

- Keeping the discussion more open-ended until it needs to advance to specific next steps.

- Using more positive, relational language instead of purely direct and factual language.

Chapter Twenty-Two

PERSONALITY AI FOR MORE SITUATIONS

We have covered a few of the most common situations where personality data can help you communicate better, but in this fast-paced, unpredictable world, there are far more types of conversations that you need to be prepared for.

While it would be impossible to create a comprehensive set of advice for every possible interaction, we have built a tool called the Conversation Coach that can help you navigate many more types of meetings, phone calls, and emails (see Figure 22.1). It allows you to select the person you need to communicate with, the mode of communication (e.g. email or call), and the specific scenario, like "resolve a conflict" or "discuss pricing."

You can find the Conversation Coach on any Crystal profile at www.crystalknows.com.

Figure 22.1 The Crystal Conversation Coach.

PART V

Lead Better

Using personality profiles to build
teams with chemistry

Chapter Twenty-Three

UNDERSTANDING THE DYNAMICS OF YOUR TEAM

Like millions of other people, one of my favorite TV shows is *The Office*. It ran for nine dramatic seasons, and its cast members have captivated fans to the point where they seem like historical figures, rather than fictional characters. Who could predict that a show about subject matter so mundane as the average workday would be so intriguing and popular, for such a long period of time?

The genius of *The Office* is in its contrasts. The physical setting appeared drab and generic on the surface, but behind the beige, corporate walls, the show's writers created a story that was rich, deep, and dramatic, even Shakespearean at times. Dunder-Mifflin, the paper company which the series is based around, portrayed a painfully normal company in a declining industry that most people never think about. But the Scranton, Pennsylvania, branch contained a diverse, vibrant mesh of personalities and intertwined relationships that we were able to watch unfold for eight consecutive years.

Looking at *The Office* through the lens of the Personality Map, it's clear why the writers never ran out of plotlines and twists to include.

Michael, the self-proclaimed "World's Best Boss" and central figure, is an off-the-charts *Motivator* (*I*). He is scatterbrained, imaginative, oddly persuasive, and at times flippant about traditions and norms. Thus, his leadership style tends to be unpredictable and polarizing, and the environment tends to be far more chaotic than the normal workplace. Every episode is a new adventure.

The rest of the characters are scattered all across the map, from other highly emotional and extroverted *I*-types like Andy (*Motivator*) and Kelly (*Encourager*) to more rigid and independent *C*-types like Oscar (*Editor*) and Angela (*Analyst*); see them all in Table 23.1. The cast seems designed for conflict. When new situations emerge, each character has a unique reaction, often in *stark* contrast to the other characters. That built-in, underlying conflict powers the show. Each new scenario brings about awkwardness, frustration, and new challenges to navigate. It's addictingly entertaining to follow, but also contains profound insights about human behavior and relationships.

The personalities of *The Office* are so well-aligned to reality that every audience member can relate to at least one of them, and when we observe their fictional daily lives it is impossible not to see a little bit of ourselves in their shoes. In case you haven't seen the show, Figure 23.1 depicts what the cast looks like on the Personality Map.

Every character has depth that makes them real and relatable. Even if you don't identify with one of them, you almost certainly know someone who does.

The show is a story about how different we are, yet how we can still find meaning and harmony together. It seems on the surface that the only thing these people have in common is the office itself—and in the early days of the show, that's largely true. When their personalities clash, it happens in natural ways that we intuitively recognize, because we have experienced the same thing in our real life. Each cast member plays a distinct archetype and presses into their most recognizable quirks and flaws, and many times the more extreme behavioral differences create inevitable conflicts. As viewers, we cannot get enough of it.

Table 23.1 Personality types of *The Office* characters.

CHARACTER	STRENGTHS	BLIND SPOTS
Michael *Motivator (I)*	Energetic, enthusiastic, visionary, emotionally sensitive, and persuasive when he needs to be.	Craves attention, impulsive, unpredictable, and at times, overbearing.
Jim *Influencer (Id)*	Charming, charismatic, quick-witted, creative, and winsome.	Can be overly sarcastic, makes jokes at the expense of others, unfocused on work at times, and distractible under stress.
Pam *Counselor (Si)*	Loyal, outgoing, friendly, and supportive.	Lacks assertiveness at times, unsure of what she wants, has goals but struggles to develop processes to achieve them.
Dwight *Skeptic (Cd)*	Industrious, relentlessly logical, competitive, and always looking to improve.	Overly intense at times, emotionally detached, distrusting of other people, and willing to put others at risk to pursue truth and order.
Angela *Analyst (C)*	Meticulous, organized, self-controlled, able to create structure and processes.	Inflexible and unwilling to adapt to others, secretive with information, highly critical of inaccuracy and inefficiency.
Phyllis *Supporter (S)*	Diplomatic in conflict, cooperative, emotionally sensitive, and trustworthy.	Can be passive aggressive under stress, sometimes allows others to take advantage of her kindness.

(continued)

Table 23.1 (continued)

CHARACTER	STRENGTHS	BLIND SPOTS
Stanley Stabilizer (SC)	Steady, reliable, comfortable complying with existing structures, traditions, and routines.	Resistant to change, forcefully responds when others push him to take action, prioritizes job security over improving performance or building relationships.
Kevin Harmonizer (IS)	Easygoing, willing to help others, friendly, cooperative.	Usually waits for others to take action instead of initiating, misses details, works at a deliberate pace.
Oscar Editor (Cs)	Detail-oriented, fair-minded, able to stay objective in conflict, reliable.	Stressed by inaccuracies, sometimes looks down on others when they make mistakes or have lower standards, hesitant to take leadership positions, even when he is well-qualified.
Kelly Encourager (Is)	Friendly, cheerful, usually has a very positive attitude, enthusiastic, and inviting towards others.	Can be emotionally volatile and very sensitive to what others think of her.
Ryan Driver (Di)	Driven, ambitious, goal-oriented, very assertive, takes action when necessary.	Insensitive to the emotions of other people, competitive to a fault, self-centered, manipulative at times.
Toby Planner (Sc)	Stable, steady, outgoing, content, cooperative.	Passive, overly permissive at times, nonconfrontational to the point of avoiding most conflicts.

Table 23.1 *(continued)*

CHARACTER	STRENGTHS	BLIND SPOTS
Creed *Initiator (DI)*	Quick on his feet and comfortable improvising, resourceful, and positive.	At times not very connected with reality, lies and embellishes the truth to get what he wants, behaves in unorthodox and strange ways.
Meredith *Initiator (DI)*	Transparent, unpredictable, fun-loving, and blunt.	Can be impolite and brash, open with information even when it is sensitive, seems aimless at times, lacks self-control.
Jan *Captain (D)*	Focused, results-oriented, fast-paced, confident, and direct in communication.	Can be controlling, overly intense, manipulative, and dominating to get what she wants.
David *Architect (Dc)*	Pragmatic, accurate, open-minded toward change when new information is available, able to look at things objectively to understand the true details of a situation.	Maintains tight control on information, at times insensitive to the emotional elements of a situation.
Andy *Motivator (I)*	Open-minded, expressive, articulate, engaging, bold, and action-oriented.	Very sensitive to how others perceive him, struggles to keep his emotions in check, and makes impulsive decisions.

Figure 23.1 The Personality Map with characters from the TV show *The Office*.

DWIGHT SCHRUTE: A CASE STUDY FOR HIGH PERFORMERS

Take Dwight Schrute, for example. He is a *Skeptic (Cd)* who sees life through a ruthlessly logical lens and always respects the rules; so much, at times, that he is willing to do things against his better judgement to conform to and enforce them. The only thing he takes more seriously than his position as the top salesman of Dunder–Mifflin is his role as a volunteer sheriff's deputy at the Scranton Police Department (often to the chagrin of the town's real police officers). He craves autonomy, and his intense, serious personality stands in direct contrast to Michael's freewheeling, emotionally volatile nature. As a result, the two often clash, with Dwight insisting that he can do a better job and Michael disregarding Dwight's very strong opinions.

Dwight's growth throughout the entire lifespan of *The Office* reads like a case study for how ambitious, independent, high-performing individual contributors can become more self-aware and balanced leaders. In the earliest seasons, Dwight is obsessed with performance and results, and he doubles down on his most raw and undeveloped impulses. He is fiercely competitive in both his job and personal life, and he generally walks around with a skeptical, calculated, "me against the world" attitude. With strong opinions, brutal objectivity, and a black-and-white worldview, he views *every* situation seriously and quickly discards anything that creates inefficiency or waste.

His seriousness also makes him very gullible, and thus vulnerable to his mischievous *Influencer (Id)* coworker, Jim Halpert. While Jim clearly respects Dwight's sales ability, he also believes that his colleague looks down on others too much, and that he sometimes acts with too much intensity and emotional detachment. So, Jim takes advantage of Dwight's tendency to ignore subtlety by staging frequent, merciless pranks.

For years, Dwight falls for these jokes as Jim continues to one-up himself. The comedic magic here comes from the huge gap between these two characters' personalities. Dwight sees Jim as a goofy, unserious salesman who doesn't have great skills beyond his ability to fly by the seat of his pants. In his view, Jim has charmed his way into unearned success, and Dwight often fantasizes about firing him once he takes over as branch manager (a career-long quest of his).

Still, Dwight's initial arrogance and overconfidence in his own opinions give him huge blind spots, which Jim exploits for his own entertainment. This battle rages back and forth throughout the duration of the show, and often seems like an eternal struggle that will never be resolved.

Dwight's relationships with both Michael and Jim seem destined for failure. How could such strong C-type qualities (logic, consistency, rigidity) ever work well together with opposing I-type qualities (expressiveness, intuition, flexibility)?

Professional relationships are unique from personal ones in that we often have far less of a choice about participating in them. If you want to hold down a job in the modern economy, you need to learn to deal with people who are different than you—sometimes extremely different. Their personalities, motivations, goals, and personal habits may seem strange or even wrong, but your success is often determined by how you reconcile those differences and work productively in spite of them. In this example from *The Office*, we witnessed a nearly decade-long transformation of Dwight from an immature, aggressive, overbearing lone wolf into a leader who could understand the emotions of others and cooperate.

In his early relationship with Michael, Dwight assumed that he knew how to do a better job than his boss, *if only* he was given the power and authority to do so. He acted as a loyal sidekick most of the time, but held onto a simmering disrespect for Michael's leadership style and apparent lack of competence. However, when Dwight achieved and squandered multiple opportunities to be a leader, he learned that many of his assumptions were wrong, and that people were not robots that he could simply program for obedience. Whereas he previously saw only the flaws in Michael's I-type tendencies, like being scatterbrained and unpredictable, he did not realize how important the I-type behaviors were for leading people—like openness to ideas and positivity. When Dwight opened the door to these new ways of thinking, he became a more dynamic, multidimensional character who was no longer held back by his blind spots.

Likewise, Michael also benefited from his working relationship with Dwight. Even though he often resisted a lot of his sidekick's more structured approaches to life, Dwight's consistency, objectivity, independence, and sense of responsibility protected the office from Michael's most disruptive impulses. Without Dwight's pragmatic, grounded nature, Michael may have created more chaos than anyone could tolerate, and the branch would be entirely dysfunctional (instead, they were one of the top-performing branches in the company). After years of working together, testing each other, and engaging in all kinds of conflicts, the two formed a close and loyal friendship that made each of them better.

Dwight's transformation was evident on a more peer-to-peer level, as well, especially in his relationship with Jim. While their daily battles continued for a long time, Dwight formed an unlikely alliance with Jim's crush/girlfriend/wife, Pam, a fellow Dunder-Mifflin employee. Pam was a strong *Counselor (Si)*, so she had a remarkable ability to perceive what other people were thinking and feeling. Having worked a few feet away from Dwight every day for years, she understood his behavior better than anyone, and often better than he did himself. Because of this, Pam was able to provide Dwight with helpful, at times secret, assistance with his people-related problems, especially his romantic ones. In this surprising friendship, Pam was able to soften Dwight's rougher edges and reveal a gentler, more compassionate person inside.

Okay, "compassionate" might be too strong of a word; Dwight was still a *Skeptic (Cd)*, laser-focused on his accomplishments and carrying out schemes to make things more efficient. By the end of the show, his core traits were very much still evident, but he interacted with others much differently. Despite the constant back-and-forth bickering with Jim, the two men slowly (*very* slowly) developed respect for each other and grew to value their relationship. At one point, Dwight stepped in to protect Jim from an attacker (Pam's ex-boyfriend) with pepper spray, and he described his act of bravery with a C-type-flavored sense of justice:

JIM: Hey man, I never got a chance to thank you . . . for stopping Roy. Thank you.

DWIGHT: Thank you not necessary and thus, not accepted. I saw someone breaking the law and I interceded.

JIM: Okay. Um... Got you something.

DWIGHT: Don't want it.

JIM: You don't know what it is.

DWIGHT: Don't want it. Won't open it. Don't need it. Won't take it. Citizens do not accept prizes for being citizens.[1]

The extreme personality traits that can make someone productive on their own are often very different from the traits that help them develop the relationships and lasting trust required to manage a team. We all have blind spots, and if we are unaware of them, those blind spots can keep us from achieving our full potential.

Dwight's story is packed with insights for high-performing individual contributors who want to become leaders. It's a grinding, at times humbling process to drag your flaws into the light and allow others to give you feedback. Instead of doubling down on his independence and self-reliance, Dwight decided to engage with others and build real relationships over time.

Not all high performers share the same intense, driving, calculated style as a young Dwight (thankfully), but we all have traits that help us more as individual contributors than as managers. Instead of assuming a team will follow the smartest, most effective, or hardest-working person in the room, we need a more nuanced approach to leadership. With accurate personality profiles, we have a way to relate to our team with more empathy and create the kind of culture that others want to be a part of.

[1] *The Office*, Season 3, Episode 18: "The Negotiation." Written by Michael Schur. Directed by Jeffrey Blitz.

Chapter Twenty-Four

FACILITATING ONE-ON-ONE CHEMISTRY BETWEEN OTHERS

To lead effectively and make wise managerial decisions, you need to understand the basics of relational dynamics. None of us exists in a vacuum. You are living in a volatile, ever-changing landscape of personalities, networks, and relational dynamics (especially if you're in a career where you need to work with other people). When you use personality assessments and AI to understand the natural dynamics *between* people, magic happens.

Usually, it takes years of trial and error to understand how you relate to another person. It takes a long time and many different situations to learn how two people handle collaboration, stress, and conflict. There's no substitute for building trust over the long-term, and there are many variables that factor into a healthy or unhealthy relationship. However, personality differences have a major impact, and if you understand the theory behind those differences, you can greatly accelerate the process.

If every relationship is its own movie, personality is the musical score that plays in the background while you watch the story unfold. The music tells you what's going on behind the dialogue between characters. It helps you understand the emotional game being played, and helps you anticipate what's coming next. If you remove the music, you can still understand the *facts* of the situation, but it's going to take much longer to understand the *feelings*.

In shorthand, we typically refer to these interpersonal dynamics as *chemistry*. In this chapter, you'll see how the Personality Map can help you understand how chemistry works across different personality types, and how you can apply this knowledge in your more important relationships.

HOW TO READ RELATIONSHIPS WITH THE PERSONALITY MAP

Navigating your network without a map can be challenging. With the Personality Map, you can understand the underlying interpersonal dynamics between any two people and work from a measurable foundation, instead of from your anecdotal observations. You simply need to know each person's natural position on the map and understand how their differences (or similarities) play out as they work together.

Vertical Distance: How Two People Naturally Collaborate

The first dimension to understand on the Personality Map is *collaboration*, which explains how easy it is for two people to work together productively. This is represented by the vertical distance between their positions on the map (see Figure 24.1).

People with personalities toward the top of the Personality Map naturally prefer to control situations and provide direction to others,

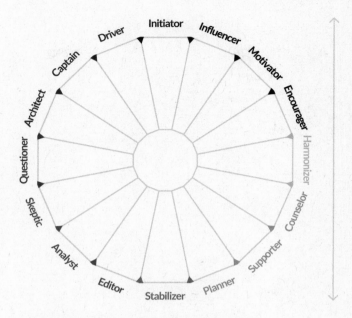

Figure 24.1 The Personality Map showing vertical distance.

while people with personalities toward the bottom of the map tend to be more comfortable following instructions, supporting others, and adapting to the environment around them.

So, the more vertical distance between two people on the map, the easier it is for them to collaborate together. The upper archetype will generally feel enough control and authority to be comfortable, while the lower archetype can feel most at ease while they react and adapt to the direction of the other person.

Note: We refer a lot to "top/upper/higher" and "bottom/lower" personality archetypes, but this is merely a way to describe the position of each dot on the map. It's not implying that one personality is better or worse than another—every archetype has its own strengths and blind spots and brings something unique to the table.

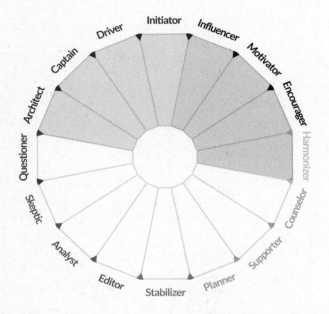

Figure 24.2 The Personality Map with the *D* and *I* regions highlighted, demonstrating a control conflict.

When two people are similarly high or low on the Personality Map, it may take more energy for them to collaborate, and will likely require them to make adjustments in order to be effective.

A *control conflict* can occur when both people have positions on the top half of the map (see Figure 24.2).

In this case, both people are likely to feel most comfortable providing direction to the other. This might play out with one person unintentionally forcing their will on the other, causing resentment and tension. Left unchecked, these types of conflicts can explode into all-out combat.

To avoid control conflicts, two upper-archetype individuals must set clear boundaries of authority and strictly respect those boundaries. Greg and I have this combination, and we both need to constantly negotiate our boundaries to stay productive (we'll get into the specifics of our personality differences later in this chapter).

On the other hand, a *control vacuum* can occur when both people have positions on the bottom half of the map (see Figure 24.3).

This interpersonal dynamic may look similar to the previous one, but it can play out very differently. Instead of competing for control, these two people may both look to the other for direction and authority. When this happens, they may become paralyzed by a big decision, or work in a way that is overly risk-averse.

Control vacuums are far less likely to result in heated arguments, but they can be just as detrimental to productivity. To avoid it, two lower-archetype individuals may need to establish (and alternate) leadership roles on specific projects, so that one person is always the clear director at any given moment, but the same person isn't forced outside of their comfort zone every single time.

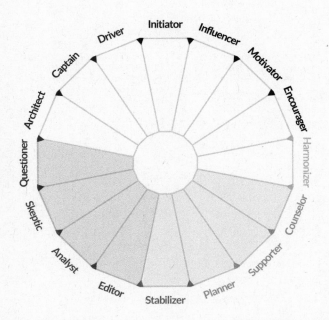

Figure 24.3 The Personality Map with the *C* and *S* regions highlighted, demonstrating a control vacuum.

Horizontal Distance: How Two People Naturally Interact

The second dimension to understand on the Personality Map is *interaction*, which explains how easy it is for two people to communicate and build trust. This is represented by the horizontal distance between their positions on the map (see Figure 24.4).

People with personalities toward the left side of the Personality Map naturally prefer independence and space in their relationships. They may be more skeptical and slow to build trust over time. Personalities toward the right side, however, tend to be more immediately trusting. They are typically perceived as warm and open when they meet new people, and may prioritize making an emotional connection.

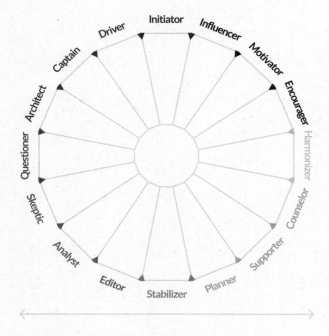

Figure 24.4 The Personality Map showing horizontal distance.

With regards to interpersonal chemistry, this works a little differently than the *collaboration* dimension. In this case, the *closer* two people are horizontally on the map, the easier it is for them to interact.

When both people are on the same horizontal side of the map, it creates *interpersonal comfort* (see Figure 24.5).

Archetypes on the left side can naturally keep conversations more formal and business-like while archetypes on the right side can approach conversations with a casual, personable demeanor to build rapport.

When both people are on opposite sides of the map, it creates *interpersonal resistance* (see Figure 24.6).

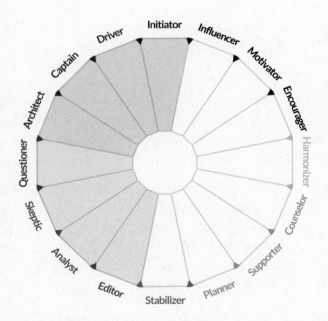

Figure 24.5 The Personality Map with the *D* and *C* regions highlighted, demonstrating interpersonal comfort.

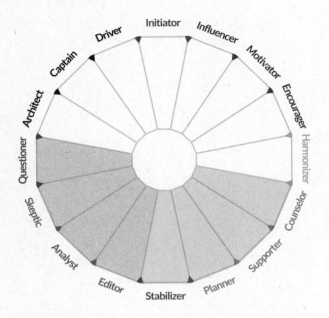

Figure 24.6 The Personality Map with the *C* and *S* regions highlighted, demonstrating interpersonal resistance.

This doesn't mean they will have friction in their relationship, necessarily. People on opposite sides of the interaction dimension can, in fact, be quite complementary. However, it does mean that they express themselves in very different ways, even if they are speaking the same language.

The resistance can come when one person in the relationship is expecting the other to communicate in the same way as them. If I'm a warmer person who likes to share friendly stories and personal connections, I may perceive someone on the left side as cold or distant. I can perceive their seriousness as an indicator that they do not like me, even if that's not what they mean at all.

Likewise, if I'm on the left side of the map and I value my independence, I may perceive someone on the right side as disingenuous, overbearing, or intrusive, when in reality they may just be asking personal questions to try and get to know me better.

Navigating Conflicts and Resistance with the Personality Map

While some personality combinations require more energy than others, they can all become healthy working relationships.

Greg and I, for example, have the odds stacked against us. I am an *Influencer (Id)* and Greg is an *Architect (Dc)*, so we are likely to experience the double whammy of *control conflicts* and *interpersonal resistance* (see Figure 24.7).

However, over the years, we have managed to build a productive, trusting, and ultimately very valuable relationship. How can that be possible with such strong differences?

Again, it comes down to *empathy*.

Figure 24.7 The Personality Map showing Greg and Drew in the *Architect* and *Influencer* regions, respectively.

267

I am a nonlinear thinker, which means that my brain comes to solutions by constantly running thought experiments and connecting dots that don't always seem connected. New ideas sprout from out of nowhere, and I spend lots of time exploring uncharted territory and seeking out exciting new concepts. As a result, my ideas do not always appear rational (they often are not) and they are not always good.

However, with that scattered mess of an imagination, I can occasionally produce something unique and valuable. I also have no problem expressing these ideas to other people and persuading them to listen. My problem, historically speaking, has been differentiating the best ideas from the shiny objects. Left unchecked, I can waste tons of time pursuing projects and initiatives that do not actually line up with reality.

As a more linear thinker, Greg is wired very differently. He is ruthlessly organized, systematic, and results-driven. This makes him an extremely effective manager, because he can hold people accountable, sniff out BS, make sure things are moving, and never let anything fall through the cracks.

However, his relentless focus on results can also cause him to miss opportunities. New ideas are never efficient, and they are usually fuzzy. If Greg is allowed to run wild, he is likely to kill those inefficient (but potentially brilliant) ideas to avoid wasting time and resources.

On top of these massive differences, toss in the fact that both of us are toward the top of the Personality Map and are only comfortable with a high level of control over our work. You can see where conflict can easily emerge.

And trust me, it does. But in spite of that natural conflict that is baked into our personalities, we have realized that we compensate for each other's blind spots very well.

For example, when one of my ideas makes it to the surface, Greg has full permission to criticize it as harshly as possible. I am biased toward optimism, so I need to run everything through Greg's brutal filter of pragmatism before it reaches the real world.

Sometimes, I need to declare a brainstorming session where the discussion needs to be less critical and more exploratory. Sometimes we end up in a fierce debate about facts, feasibility, and underlying assumptions. Usually, we end up with a much better, more polished idea.

This constant battle makes both of us better, and we have built a foundation of long-term trust as a result of it. If two people with such extreme, conflicting personalities can make it work, anyone can.

Chapter Twenty-Five

CREATING CHEMISTRY WITHIN AN ENTIRE GROUP

If one-on-one relationships have so much going on beneath the surface, imagine how infinitely complex an entire group of people can be. With so many conflicting personalities and competing motivations, it's a miracle for any team of people to decide on a shared goal and make progress toward it.

Yet, we work in *companies*, live in *communities*, and bind ourselves together as *families*. Group dynamics are at play in most areas of social and professional life, so it is well worth your time to understand how groups work. Or, you can shoot from the hip and hope that you continue getting invited to dinner parties. The choice is yours.

WHY GROUPS ARE SO HARD TO DEAL WITH

There's a concept in software engineering called Brooks's Law, more commonly known as the "Mythical Man-Month." This law observes that adding more people to a project actually causes the project to take *longer* to complete.

This goes against common sense logic. If a project with two engineers was supposed to take eight weeks, shouldn't four engineers be able to complete the project in half the time?

If you have ever been involved in the product development process, you know that the answer is a resounding "no." While there are many reasons this occurs, the root cause has to do with the math of group intercommunication.

The group intercommunication formula looks like this:

$$n(n-1)/2 = x$$

In this formula, n is the number of people in the group, and x is the number of communication channels in the group.

Let's use that previous example, with two engineers:

$$2(2-1)/2 = 1 \text{ relationship}$$

With two people, you only have one communication channel to manage (see Figure 25.1). This is the simplest group, because everyone in the group has full insight into all of the communication in the group. Nothing falls through the cracks, nobody feels ignored, and nobody talks behind someone else's back (no, it doesn't count when we quietly mumble curse words to ourselves while debugging JavaScript).

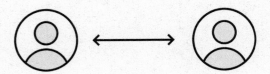

Figure 25.1 With two people, there is one relationship to manage.

What happens when we expand the team to four engineers?

$$4(4-1)/2 = 6 \text{ relationships}$$

Whoa. Adding two more people to the team actually added *five* more communication channels (see Figure 25.2). That's five more relationships to manage, five more opportunities for miscommunication, five more opportunities for egos to brush up against each other.

In addition, now everyone on the team has multiple lines of communication that they are cut out of by default (see Figure 25.2). Engineer A has full view of her interactions with Engineer B and Engineer C, but no idea what Engineer B and C are saying to each other. To get that information, she needs to stop what she's doing, ask for it, and then rely on others to deliver it accurately.

You can now see why this project timeline would not shrink from eight to four weeks. In fact, it's likely to grow beyond eight weeks.

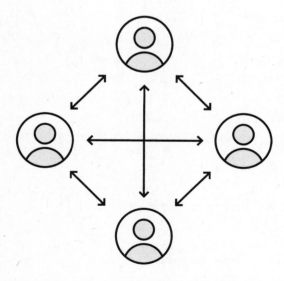

Figure 25.2 With four people, there are six relationship to manage.

As a thought experiment, let's see what happens when we expand the team to 10 people . . .

$$10(10-1)/2 = 45 \text{ relationships}$$

With 10 engineers, the group explodes to 45 communication channels (see Figure 25.3). Even the most diligent, organized, engaging manager cannot handle that kind of workload without missing things.

With 45 communication channels, breakdowns are highly likely, if not inevitable. However, if you understand how personality differences affect group dynamics, you can spot those breakdowns where they

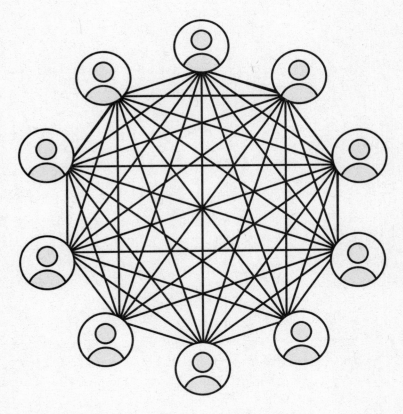

Figure 25.3 With 10 people, there are 45 relationship to manage.

happen, whether it's on a software team, in a board meeting, or at the dinner table.

UNDERSTANDING COMPLEX RELATIONSHIPS WITHIN A GROUP

Personality differences are evenly distributed across the population, and we believe this is indicative of something important:

We need to balance each other out to survive.

Because every human has blind spots, we need to be around people with different strengths to fill in our gaps. If we only associate with those who think like us, we will compound our weaknesses and ultimately fail. There is beauty in diversity of thought, and a healthy, functional group knows how to maintain balance and harness the differences between people.

I am the oldest of four children in my family. The D'Agostino house was a melting pot of personalities growing up, and it looked something like the breakdown in Figure 25.4.

From a quick glance at the Personality Map, you can understand a few important things:

- As a group, the D'Agostino family mostly clusters on the top half of the map. That means most of us tend to be more extraverted, and we tend to value both decision-making authority and control of their environment. This creates lots

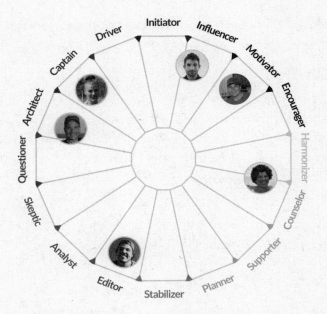

Figure 25.4 The Personality Map showing Drew's family members.

of control conflicts, which usually happen out in the open with verbal debate.

- My brother Evan is largely alone in the bottom left region, which means he is far and away the most logical and analytical one of the bunch. When the rest of the family shouts out their latest political views or bad jokes at dinner time, he could sit by and silently watch, content with his spaghetti, meatballs, and quiet curiosity.

- My brother Josh and my mom are solidly on the right side of the map, so their relationship tends to be more animated, emotional, and open. They talk frequently and are very verbal with their feelings.

- My sister Joanna and my dad are also very close on the map, but they're over on the left side. They have a respectful, direct relationship where each can communicate sharply or even bluntly without getting offended.

These are all things that my family knows intuitively as a result of living together for most of our lives. But when we put everyone on the map and talked through the results for the first time, it provided a language to describe the underlying dynamics that we had been subtly feeling—and answer questions that had been weighing on us—for all those years.

There are conflicts, of course, but now we have the language to address issues in an objective, nonconfrontational way.

Chapter Twenty-Six

BECOMING AN EMPATHY-DRIVEN LEADER

Working with a team (or interacting with your family) is difficult enough, with all of the intertwined relationships, competing incentives, and random situations that life throws at each person. However, it's an entirely different ballgame when you're responsible for the group as a whole, and that requires a special skill set.

There are, of course, many aspects to effective leadership. Most of these general lessons are well-researched, thoroughly explored for hundreds of years, and assembled into clean, organized handbooks that are available with one click. However, most leaders still struggle and many fail to retain their team members (the phrase "Employees don't quit their job, they quit their boss" comes to mind). It's because groups of people are endlessly complex, and boilerplate advice is not enough. Truly great leaders are able to absorb the broad, tried-and-true bits of management wisdom and apply them to the unique dynamics of their team.

Personality differences often drive these dynamics. In high-pressure environments, those differences can create rifts, misalignment, and unpredictability. To navigate successfully, a leader must be first aware of the strengths, blind spots, and motivations of each person on their team—starting with themselves.

Brian Halligan and Dharmesh Shah, the founders of HubSpot who serve as the company's CEO and CTO, respectively, have built a business with over 56,000 customers, 2,000 employees, and over $500 million in annual revenue.[1] HubSpot went public in 2014, and since then, the stock price has increased by more than 500%.[2] By any business measure, these two have succeeded as leaders.

Yet, their leadership styles could not appear more different. Brian is an outspoken, animated risk-seeker[3] who frequently cuts against conventional wisdom and paid $1.9 million for a Grateful Dead guitar. Dharmesh is a self-proclaimed introvert[4] who hates small talk, intentionally shuns phone calls, and tries to write code every day.[5] If there was a standard "personality of a leader," these two have proven it wrong.

Leadership at any level of scale is tough. In the case of a rapidly growing company, it can feel like assembling a plane while you're already rolling forward on the runway. You need to make huge decisions with limited information, build a machine that can actually fly, keep enough gas in the tank, and pray that you take off before you run out of pavement. Every problem seems different than the last and requires a different skill to solve,

[1] Dharmesh Shah, "The Hubspot Culture Code: Creating a Company We Love," *HubSpot*, July 10, 2018, updated July 15, 2018, https://blog.hubspot.com/blog/tabid/6307/bid/34234/the-hubspot-culture-code-creating-a-company-we-love.aspx.
[2] Hubspot Inc. Stock Quote (U.S.: NYSE), https://www.marketwatch.com/investing/stock/hubs.
[3] Interview with Brian Halligan, CEO and Co-Founder of Hub Spot, *MIT Entrepreneurship Review*, May 24, 2011, http://miter.mit.edu/articleinterview-brian-halligan-ceo-co-founder-hub-spot.
[4] Dharmesh Shah, "Sorry, No Calls," OnStartups, November 20, 2012, https://www.onstartups.com/tabid/3339/bid/92302/Sorry-No-Calls.aspx.
[5] Larry Kim, "23 Amazing Facts About HubSpot's Dharmesh Shah," *Inc.*, May 16, 2016, https://www.inc.com/larry-kim/23-amazing-facts-about-hubspots-dharmesh-shah.html.

so a leadership team needs to shift their behaviors all over the Personality Map. This is why a solo leader can feel like they need to *be* so many different people—the pilot, mechanic, and navigator—all at once. Two people, on the other hand, can balance each other out, so they're slightly more likely to get off the ground.

Leading a team, or an entire organization for that matter, can be a frustratingly complex job. Luckily, the HubSpot founders have shared their formula for all of us to read. While it is not a template, it mentions some key foundational principles that Personality AI can help us implement.

In 2013, Dharmesh published the *HubSpot Culture Code*,[6] a slide deck explaining precisely what the company believes and how its team works together. It emphasized the core idea that "culture doesn't just help attract amazing people, it amplifies their abilities and helps them do their best work."

After a 2018 revision,[7] he added a core value: *empathy*.

With empathy at the center of the culture, Dharmesh and Brian set the expectation that their team would "not only see things from the other person's perspective, but approach things from that person's perspective." This meant understanding the true needs and motivations of customers, as well as hiring people who had the ability to see things through someone else's eyes.

From the stock price, the explosive growth, and the consistent ranking as one of the *Best Places to Work*, we can see that this approach has created massive value for HubSpot. Leading with empathy takes intentional planning and focus. It is not always the most convenient way to interact, nor is it always the most cost-effective in the short-term. However, using personality data makes it more feasible in day-to-day life as a leader.

---

[6] Shah, "The HubSpot Culture Code."
[7] Dharmesh Shah, "How We Fixed a Critical Bug in HubSpot's Culture Code," *HubSpot*, February 15, 2018, https://www.hubspot.com/careers-blog/how-we-fixed-a-critical-bug-in-hubspots-culture-code.

UNDERSTANDING YOUR LEADERSHIP STYLE ———

From the previous chapters, you already know that you have strengths and blind spots. In a leadership position, they become magnified. Your actions have a disproportionate impact on everyone else, so problems that you can sweep under the rug as an individual contributor can quickly blossom into big, glorious, mission-threatening conflicts.

Personality insights can help you avoid these eruptions. More frequently, they can help you quickly deal with the parade of micro-conflicts that you encounter every day before they get a chance to grow. It might be the fleeting passive aggressive comment from one team member to another, or the repeated request for a more flexible schedule, or the empty "fine" that someone gives you when you ask how they are doing. Having quick access to accurate personality data and real-time advice can help you push the right buttons in each of these scenarios.

However, you have some prep work to do first. Before you try understanding the personality tendencies of your team, and before you use powerful tools like assessments and AI to improve their performance, you need an accurate assessment of your own personality.

This level of self-awareness will make all of the later interactions with your team more effective, because it requires you to start from a place of honesty. With brutal honesty about your own shortcomings, you can be open and empathetic toward your team instead of accusatory and demanding. It creates an objective no-judgement zone, where each party is free to discuss how they *really* feel about their performance, tasks, and responsibilities.

For this leadership self-assessment, we will use the Personality Map again. Each archetype leads with a very different style (see Table 26.1), which impacts factors like team structure, time expectations, communication preferences, and overall culture. By knowing your natural style, you can anticipate how your team already perceives you and identify where you may need some counterweight.

Table 26.1 Leadership styles for each personality type.

ARCHETYPE	LEADERSHIP STYLE
D: Architects, Captains, Drivers, Initiators	• Eager to take charge and provide clear direction. • Tends to challenge others with demanding tasks and high expectations. • Provides high-level instructions that focus on the end result. • Creates a competitive, dynamic work environment.
I: Influencers, Motivators, Encouragers, Harmonizers	• Creates a casual, outgoing work environment. • Focused on inspiring others with a bold vision of the future. • More comfortable delivering important messages verbally, with group meetings. • Gives others autonomy to find their own solutions to problems.
S: Counselors, Supporters, Planners, Stabilizers	• Typically leads by example. • Creates a peaceful, calm work environment. • Expects team members to be stable, reliable, and cooperative. • Focused on developing the team with one-on-one coaching and instruction.

(continued)

Table 26.1 *(continued)*

ARCHETYPE	LEADERSHIP STYLE
C: Editors, Analysts, Skeptics, Questioners	• More comfortable distributing important messages in writing. • Focused on creating rules and processes for others to follow. • Expects team members to make decisions with logic and supporting data. • Provides detailed, specific instructions to solve problems.

Your strengths as a leader are helpful to know and fun to write on your resumé, but the real value in knowing your natural archetype is getting exposed to your blind spots.

Your team can likely already describe your leadership style accurately, but you may not be getting the whole story. When someone relies on you for a paycheck, it may be difficult to pry out this information from them. They may complain about your blind spots to their friends, they but are unlikely to risk offending you by sharing them openly in a one-on-one meeting.

This is another place where Personality AI—and personality data more broadly—gives you an unfair advantage as a leader. Machines are not susceptible to the situational emotions or risks involved in pointing out where you may be weak. They give you the cold, calculated results even when they are not flattering.

Dealing with your blind spots as a leader may require you to shine a bright light on them (see Table 26.2). Personality AI shows you where to point the flashlight. When you do so, you open up a world of transparency with your team, and you can have much easier, more

Table 26.2 Leadership blind spots for each personality type.

ARCHETYPE	LEADERSHIP BLIND SPOTS
D: Architects, Captains, Drivers, Initiators	• Work environment might feel overly competitive or aggressive to some people. • May immediately resolve conflict with outward verbal disputes. • Pace of work may be too fast for team members to complete their tasks with high enough quality for their standards. • May not allow team members enough flexible time to get to know each other well and build trust. • May make changes suddenly, without fully informing the team or providing enough time to prepare.
I: Influencers, Motivators, Encouragers, Harmonizers	• May not maintain thorough notes and documentation for team members to refer to. • May have a relaxed attitude toward risks, without carefully considering the costs and consequences of major decisions. • May not devote enough time for the team to analyze the details of a problem before jumping to solutions. • May not detect or seek out underlying problems before they become obvious. • May lead the team to pursue multiple goals at once when more focus is required.

(continued)

Table 26.2 (continued)

ARCHETYPE	LEADERSHIP BLIND SPOTS
S: Counselors, Supporters, Planners, Stabilizers	• May be overly forgiving instead of holding team members accountable to deadlines, quality, and responsibilities. • May only see the best in people when more skepticism or criticism is needed. • Decisions may be difficult when lots of people with conflicting interests are involved. • May allow interpersonal conflicts to sit beneath the surface without bringing them out into the open. • May miss out on good opportunities for team development and advancement because of high sensitivity to risk.
C: Editors, Analysts, Skeptics, Questioners	• Team members may not feel emotionally connected and engaged. • May encourage the team to spend lots of time researching and assembling information when immediate action is required. • Might ignore the emotional or social impact of a decision, even when it is logical and practical. • May be overly strict in creating and enforcing rules. • May restrict more creative team members by requiring them to conform with standard practices, rather than allowing for flexibility.

productive conversations about how everyone can function better together as a unit.

If you understand how your own personality tendencies will drive you to behave, you can know where you are likely to get resistance or pushback from your team. You should give them access to those blind spots—doing so will prevent unnecessary stress, interpersonal tension, and decision paralysis.

SETTING OTHERS UP FOR SUCCESS

Each person on your team has a unique blend of desires, motivations, and behavioral tendencies. As we illustrated earlier, a team of 10 is actually made up of 45 different relationships that need to be managed, each with its own history and chemistry.

While it is impossible to understand all of the complex interactions happening on a team of more than two people, the Personality Map can show you how to put each team member into a *position* to thrive without micromanagement. Natural personality types all play differently with each other, so you want to know where each person sits relative to you, their colleagues, their everyday tasks, and their work environment as a whole.

Adapting to Your Team's Work Style Preferences

Let's say you're managing a *Captain (D)* named Melissa. She's more assertive than most people, competitive, ambitious, and unafraid to ruffle feathers from time to time. Since you are similarly wired, you may both be very comfortable with direct feedback, regularly criticizing each other with harsher language and getting right to the point.

However, you also may have others on your team who are *Planners*, *Counselors*, and other archetypes who are less confrontational, and may be turned off by such bluntness. If you lead them in the same way that you lead Melissa, you'll have problems.

In this case, understanding someone's personality can help you choose your words more wisely, and Personality AI can automate the process. In Crystal, you can view *work style preferences* for how someone is likely to receive feedback best, resolve conflict, and collaborate with others.

For example, Table 26.3 shows what the preferences look like for a *Captain (D)* like Melissa.

Table 26.3 Communication preferences for a Captain.

ACTIVITY	CAPTAIN PREFERENCE
Meetings	Meetings should be very quick, to the point, and only scheduled when necessary.
Email	Emails should be brief, business-like, and concise.
Feedback	Feedback should be candid, direct, and focused on the most important points.
Conflict	Conflict is essential for improvement, as long as it is actionable and objective.
Teamwork	Teams should have a leader with clearly defined authority and effective distribution of responsibilities.

Creating an Energizing Work Environment

Beyond your one-on-one relationship with each person, your responsibilities also may extend to which tasks they are assigned, who they work with, and the culture in which they work. The *Captain (D)*, Melissa, may be energized or drained by very different things than her colleagues, and if you know this information, you can put her in a position where she is most productive.

Table 26.4 shows what an *energizing* work environment looks like for a *Captain (D)* while Table 26.5 demonstrates a draining work environment.

Table 26.4 An energizing work environment for a Captain.

YOUR BOSS	YOUR PEERS	YOUR DIRECT REPORTS
• Sets high expectations for your performance.	• Communicate bluntly with each other in a business-like tone.	• Ask you for help clearing obstacles, rather than step-by-step guidance.
• Pushes you to improve.	• Are able to "agree to disagree" instead of compromising on every decision.	• Work well with clear goals and the freedom to achieve them independently.
• Allows you to compete with other people.		
• Gives you a high degree of autonomy.	• Engage in lively, spirited debate.	• Quickly vocalize concerns, delays, and potential issues.
• Offers clear, direct feedback.	• Compliment your high level thinking with detail-oriented feedback.	• Independently create solutions and present them to the group.
	• Diagnose potential problems with your work.	• Separate emotions from their decision-making.

Predicting Personality

Table 26.5 A draining work environment for a Captain.

YOUR BOSS	YOUR PEERS	YOUR DIRECT REPORTS
• Speaks too passively when providing instructions or feedback.	• Spend more time talking about ideas and theories rather than taking action.	• Take a long time to complete tasks.
• Does not provide clear goals or problems to solve.	• Avoid conflict and let interpersonal issues simmer beneath the surface.	• Require your approval for every decision, even small ones.
• Creates a rigid set of rules for you to follow.	• Require a lot of approval and buy-in before moving forward with a task.	• Provide long, detailed written reports rather than succinct ones.
• Does not give you ownership over a project that you're working on.	• Shy away from critical feedback.	• Rely heavily on group collaboration.
• Seems indecisive or noncommittal.	• Ask you to slow down your pace of work.	• Value stability and security over progress.

View work style preferences, energizers, stressors, and more in the Crystal Full Personality Report, which can be accessed from crystalknows.com.

BUILDING TEAMS WITH CHEMISTRY

Company culture has become an overused buzzword for a reason—it really makes a difference. When teams gel, they can produce much more than the sum of each person's individual contribution. Good chemistry allows a group to punch above its weight class.

When you're in the powerful position to start a team from scratch, or add to an existing team, it can be daunting. You may go through five or six rounds of interviews, and still feel like you're gambling with the future.

And statistically, you usually are. The average U.S.-based company turned over 44.3% percent of its workforce in 2018.[8] Firms in especially low-retention industries like entertainment and hospitality replace more than 75% of their employees annually, while a "high-retention" industry like technology hovers around 35%. In a 2018 study,[9] Deloitte found that 43% of millennials expect to leave their job within two years and over 70% expect to leave within five years.

The good news is, you probably have a lot of opportunity to increase productivity and reduce turnover-related costs. The bad news? As evidenced by a multitude of reports[10] about our increasingly job-hopping culture, long-lasting and productive teams are exceptionally rare (and getting rarer). But with Personality AI, you can face this challenge with a full arsenal of data and give your team the unfair advantage of *built-in empathy*.

---

[8] Annual total separations rates by industry and region, not seasonally adjusted, https://www.bls.gov/news.release/jolts.t16.htm.
[9] Deloitte, *Millennial Survey 2018*, Social impact, Innovation, https://www2.deloitte.com/global/en/pages/about-deloitte/articles/millennialsurvey.html.
[10] Gallup, Inc., "Millennials: The Job-Hopping Generation," https://www.gallup.com/workplace/231587/millennials-job-hopping-generation.aspx.

Choosing the Right Team at the Right Time

Just like there are no "good" or "bad" relational matches on the Personality Map, there are no good or bad group combinations. Every group has a unique dynamic, each with its own benefits and risks.

The key is to understand what the benefits and risks are by analyzing the personalities within the group, then making sure they are aligned with your overall goals. Let's go through some examples.

D-heavy Culture: The Pressure-Cooker

If you're in a cutthroat industry, where competition is fierce and the winner takes all, you may need to stack your team in a more aggressive, dominant direction.

It may be necessary to set up a more competitive environment where people can demand excellence and openly challenge each other to improve. To accomplish that, you would want to bring in more *Architects, Captains, Drivers,* and *Initiators,* who sit toward the top left of the Personality Map (see Figure 26.1).

While you will likely incur the benefits of a highly driven group that can move fast to achieve results, you may also open yourself up to risks like:

- Frequent verbal conflict.

- Struggles over control.

- Aggressive, workaholic-like behavior.

This type of group dynamic typically works best when the team is more of a collection of individual contributors who do not necessarily need to collaborate or cooperate with each other very often.

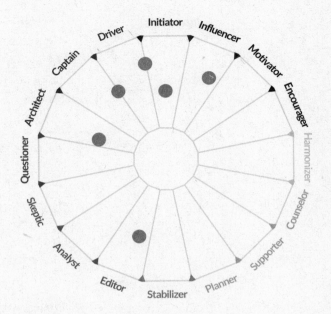

Figure 26.1 The Personality Map with clustering around *D* personalities.

I-heavy Culture: The Sandbox

Some industries and companies require a more creative, flexible approach to work. In these cases, it may be best to add more *Influencers, Motivators, Encouragers* and *Harmonizers* from the top right of the Personality Map (see Figure 26.2).

These teams will tend to be welcoming to new people and ideas. They may be very collaborative, open, and emotionally driven.

These groups can be extremely innovative, and they may create inspiring, revolutionary products. At the same time, they may:

- Chase "shiny objects" instead of focusing on one thing and following through to completion.

- Decide to make changes quickly, without doing enough research.

Figure 26.2 The Personality Map with clustering around *I* personalities.

- Operate with a very loose sense of rules and expectations, so goals may be unclear and processes can become disorganized.

In situations where diligence, caution, and precision are required, this type of group may struggle. However, when you can afford to take big, bold risks and explore uncharted territory without being too efficient, it can be ideal.

S-heavy culture: The Sanctuary

In mature companies that have built a steady operation that needs to be carefully maintained, it may be beneficial to fill the team with *Counselors*, *Supporters*, *Planners*, and *Stabilizers* (see Figure 26.3).

These teams tend to prioritize stability, reliability, and careful planning. They often value collaboration and avoiding conflict or "rocking the boat."

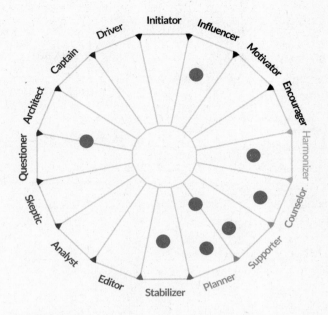

Figure 26.3 The Personality Map with clustering around *S* personalities.

In an *S*-heavy team, the organization is unlikely to rush into decisions or react impulsively to market conditions. At the same time, they may:

- Make decisions too slowly, missing the bigger picture.

- Be hesitant to remove poor performing team members.

- Miss out on innovation because of a focus on maintaining the status quo.

This type of group is best suited for an organization and market that is well-established and is playing defense to protect well-built competitive advantages, rather than frequently creating new products.

C-heavy Culture: The Laboratory

If you want to create a hyper-meticulous, highly pragmatic environment where people encourage each other to triple-check all of their work and avoid mistakes, you will want more C-types in the room, such as *Skeptics*, *Analysts*, and *Editors* (see Figure 26.4).

A C-focused team places a high value on accuracy and quality, likely creating stable, dependable products that get the job done right. For example, if you are building a bridge that needs to hold up thousands of cars and pedestrians each day without collapsing, you'll want plenty of C personalities present.

While a group with many C personalities can be relied upon to solve complex problems, they may run into issues when they:

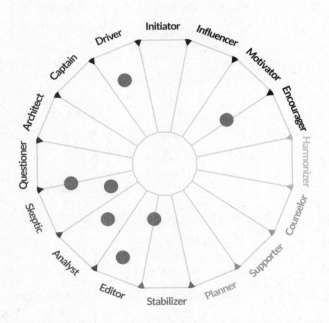

Figure 26.4 The Personality Map with clustering around C personalities.

- Restrict innovation and creativity in order to reduce risk.

- Spend too much time analyzing options and delay decision-making.

- Focus too much on efficiency and ignore the emotions of others.

A team of *C* personalities can be well-suited to figure out difficult challenges and account for the many details that others might miss.

Balanced Culture: The Melting Pot

Sometimes, you need a team that can straddle the line between risk and reward, boldness and caution.

Whether it's the board of a public company, a congressional caucus, or a trivia team, you will want to make sure to include an even distribution of personality archetypes, without skewing too far in any direction on the Personality Map (see Figure 26.5).

Rather than finding people who are as close to each other on the Personality Map as possible, you want to find people who balance each other out. If you have a strong *Captain (D)*, you need a strong *Supporter (S)*. If you have an extreme *Initiator (DI)*, you need an extreme *Stabilizer (SC)*. These archetypes have complementary traits, which can ultimately lead to better, wiser decisions.

However, balance is not a cure for all of your group collaboration challenges. It has risks, just like any other team, including:

- Internal miscommunication, with so many different styles at play.

- Conflicting motivations between group members.

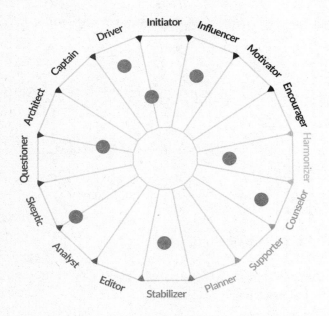

Figure 26.5 The Personality Map with a melting pot of different personalities.

- Impulse for the strong *D*-types to take a controlling position.

In balanced teams, leaders need to be vocal and specific about cultural norms and expectations. Sometimes, the group will need to adopt *S*-like caution, while at other times more aggressive *D*-like behavior may be necessary.

FILLING IN GAPS ON YOUR TEAM

Suppose you have a product designer who is a *Motivator*, or a strong *I* personality. She is fantastic when it comes to brainstorming new ideas, creatively illustrating mockups and pushing the limits in exciting ways when designing a new product. However, what happens if your team enters a season where you aren't creating anything new, and instead are making slow, incremental, and detailed adjustments to the product you already have? This product designer could certainly do that work, but in order to do so, she is going to be driving far from home on the Personality Map every day. Her personality will crave new, exciting, creative work.

When you come across a situation like this product designer, you've encountered a classic dilemma where the personalities on your team do not match the goal you are trying to achieve. In this case, your team may be much better served by an *S*-type or *C*-type designer, who is exceptional at detailed, incremental adjustments rather than one who is constantly eager to create bold new layouts.

In order to determine the optimal personality type for a role, we use Crystal's Role Survey tool. To use the tool, a team leader and coworkers rank a set of behaviors on a scale of Important to Neutral to Unimportant. Each behavior corresponds to a certain personality type. For example, "working methodically and focusing on details" is a behavior most likely associated with *C*-type personalities. Once we select the behaviors that are the most and least important for a role, we use Crystal to analyze the results and identify a suggested archetype. We then can compare potential candidates to the ideal personality archetype we identified, and see how they match up.

Personality should not be the only factor used to make hiring decisions, nor do we advocate directly excluding someone because their personality misaligns with the behaviors you identified were most important for a role. However, seeing personality match or mismatch can give you an idea of important questions to discuss in an interview. For example, if it doesn't come naturally for someone's personality type to pay attention to detail, perhaps they have recognized that blind spot and purposely have worked to become more detail-oriented in their career.

START UNDERSTANDING YOUR TEAM BETTER ————

If this idea—using personality profiles to build a stronger team, improve your team chemistry, and set up your team for success—resonates with you, we recommend that you sign up for Crystal (www.crystalknows .com/personality) and invite your team to create their own personality profiles. Each person gets free access to insights for every employee in their company, including communication style, work preferences, situation-specific coaching, and more.

PART VI

Predict Responsibly

Understanding the proper, ethical use
of Personality AI

Chapter Twenty-Seven

HOW TO PROPERLY USE PERSONALITY DATA

Soon after we launched our first product in 2015, the technology press started to get curious. As the CEO, I took all of the interviews I could with online publications, podcasts, and radio shows. We had some wonderful, productive conversations about personality profiles and using empathy to improve communication, and we shared all we could about how Crystal worked. It was invigorating to bring this message to the world and explain how personality data could help people be more connected and engaged with each other in the future.

Yet, we were surprised when we saw the salacious slant of some of the headlines. A few referred to us as "creepy" or implied that we were "getting inside your head." It was enough to get our attention and rethink our messaging, because the world was clearly skeptical.

Even though our product was using personality models that had been around for thousands of years and only drawing inferences from publicly available data, the results were often so accurate that they could feel invasive. Most of our users understood the functionality of our products, but for those who didn't, it could seem like Crystal was somehow accessing people's secrets and making them available for anyone willing to pay us. How else could a company get such accurate psychographic information?

In the years after, the public conversation around data privacy and AI quickly accelerated. In the United States, Facebook become embroiled in controversy after allowing a private company, Cambridge Analytica, to analyze data from millions of users for political campaigns. In Europe, the EU passed a sweeping new data privacy law called the General Data Protection Regulation (GDPR),[1] requiring all companies who handle the personal data of EU citizens to follow strict guidelines for processing and storing the data. Companies who violated these new data privacy rights would be subject to massive fines (up to $20MM). This was soon followed with similar legislation in California.[2]

As soon as we understood the skepticism around personality data and the global regulatory trends, we decided to make trust and transparency a key pillar of our strategy. We knew that Personality AI could be of enormous benefit to society by enabling empathy, communication, and new relationships, but if we did not explain it correctly, it could be perceived as invasive, manipulative, or, as those articles so eloquently put it, *creepy*.

SCIENCE FICTION VERSUS REALITY

Most of the skepticism around Personality AI, at least in the case of Crystal, comes from confusion around what it actually is. When people see a personality profile without any context, they can let their imaginations run wild to a futuristic dystopia—the kind where you get a government-issued chip in your arm and send a constant stream of data to Big Brother.

Thankfully, this isn't the case. Personality AI simply reads a set of existing data, tries to understand what it means, and uses it to generate a

---

[1] The EU General Data Protection Regulation (GDPR) Is the Most Important Change in Data Privacy Regulation in 20 Years, https://eugdpr.org.
[2] California Consumer Privacy Act, https://www.caprivacy.org.

probability that something may or may not happen in the future. To understand the limits, we need clear definitions:

Personality AI is:

- A technique to determine the probability that someone may exhibit certain behavioral tendencies, based on things we know about people who have similar assessment responses, text samples, and other qualities.

- A way to learn a person's preferred communication style to maximize the chance that they understand your message and engage in conversation.

- An effective method for opening up discussions between people about their professional or personal relationship.

- A tool for understanding the overall behavioral dynamics within a group of people.

Personality AI is not:

- Capable of understanding anything about a person outside of general conclusions that can be drawn from trends in its existing dataset.

- Able to deliver psychographic information that can or should be presented as absolute facts.

- A tool for coercion or manipulation of individuals.

- An effective substitute for asking questions and learning more about other people.

Now, despite the technical limits of data Personality AI can realistically generate, there is still a burden of responsibility on the user to utilize the data it *can* generate in an ethical, transparent, and compliant way.

RESPECTING DATA PRIVACY

Like any artificial intelligence, Personality AI is an engine fueled by data and it always wants more of it. Since technology is amoral, it does not care where the data came from, who owns it, how high the quality is, or who can be affected by it. Only the human that builds, trains, and uses the AI can decide what *acceptable* or *unacceptable* data is. As professionals with access to this powerful technology, it's on us to understand the difference.

When we train AI and use the results to make some kind of decision, we need to distinguish between *anonymous* and *personal* data. We also need to have a strong, consistent philosophy of data ownership so it is crystal clear what we should protect, analyze, publish, and share.

Anonymous Data

While most data in the public domain has been provided by *some* human, a dataset is considered *anonymous* for our purposes when you cannot tie the individual records to specific people. Because of that, anonymous data cannot negatively impact any individual person and has far less regulation than personal data.

In the world of AI, anonymous data is used extensively to train algorithms. Crystal, for example, uses an aggregated set of personality assessment results to understand how personality traits cluster together (helping us identify our 16 personality archetypes instead of an infinite number of random behaviors). Training data like this does not have identifying information attached, so it can be analyzed and published without restriction.

With millions of personality assessment responses, we can find population-level trends like "software engineers tend to be more logical" and "sales representatives tend to be more outgoing" and support those observations with real data. This allows us to continue improving the AI, yielding more accurate results and more value for end users in the future.

Personal Data

Most of the regulations around data privacy involve personal data. As people put more and more of their lives online, they have put a great deal of trust in the companies who handle their precious information. The newly enacted data law from the European Union, GDPR (General Data Protection Regulation), provides rules and guidelines for these companies. The law defines personal data as "any information relating to an identified or identifiable natural person."

Furthermore . . .

> An identifiable natural person is one who can be identified, directly or indirectly, in particular by reference to an identifier such as a name, an identification number, location data, an online identifier or to one or more factors specific to the physical, physiological, genetic, mental, economic, cultural or social identity of that natural person.

Since Personality AI deals with psychographic analysis on the *individual* level, it is clearly working within the scope of personal data. This data can include:

- Training datasets like personality assessment results and text samples.

- Potentially identifying attributes like job title, employer, industry, and location.

- User provided information like email, name, company, and behavioral characteristics.

THREE RULES FOR DATA PRIVACY

Designing a product like Crystal has led us to set up clear boundaries around our data, both for our users and for the people that they analyze. We have formalized these boundaries into three rules, so our users can clearly understand the core philosophy driving our decisions.

Be Clear and Forthcoming about What Personal Data Is Used For

Put simply, users should know what they are getting themselves into. This rule is not exclusive to Personality AI by any means, but since we are working in a particularly *personal* realm, it means our users have a particularly close attachment to the data they provide and how it is used.

Only Use Data That You Have Permission to Access

While an algorithm doesn't have any legal obligations, ethical standards, or emotional attachments to the data it analyzes, real people do.

Some information, like an article someone writes, is clearly and unambiguously in the public domain, and thus available for collection and analysis. Other information is obviously private and protected, like someone's electronic medical records or bank account balance. However, there is a huge swath of data between those extremes and we need more guidance to understand where the line is between *usable* and *unusable*. One example is email content.

While an email can sometimes be covered by copyright laws,[3] the recipient of an email can read and analyze its contents. Many companies have conducted studies by aggregating email data to understand correlations, and provide insights about how to run more productive campaigns.[4] In our case, email data can be very useful

---

[3] Northeastern University Law Review, "Do Not Forward: Why Passing Along an Email May Constitute Copyright Infringement," http://nulawreview.org/extralegalrecent/do-not-forward-why-passing-along-an-email-may-constitute-copyright-infringement.
[4] Elise Musumano, "386 Million Emails Reveal Benchmark Email Productivity and Engagement," https://www.yesware.com/blog/benchmark-email.

for predicting the personality type of the author, which can be used to generate personal communication insights.

However, *reading* and *analyzing* an email is not the same as *publishing* it. When we generate personality insights from an email text sample, we are creating a new piece of *inferred* or *derived data*, which should be treated with just as much care and diligence as ordinary personal data. And that brings us to the next rule. . .

Only Publish Data with Consent

We should not only be asking what standards we are legally required to comply with, but what standards our customers want us to hold with their data.

As we pointed out, lots of personal data is available for consuming and repurposing. Many companies provide this service, aggregating public data and organizing it for other businesses to enrich their customer databases and enhance their products.

Derived personal data, like a personality profile, is a different class of information, especially when it comes from sources that are not publicly available. Since Personality AI makes *predictions* about someone, it makes statements that are, by definition, sometimes incorrect. That's why you'll notice lots of qualifying language in Crystal, like "this person tends to . . ." or "is likely to . . ."

The legal standards for publishing derived personal data are still relatively unclear, and they vary from country to country. At Crystal, we have adopted the overall policy of *not publishing any personality data derived from non-public personal data, without the consent of the person*.

That's a mouthful, but it means that if a personality profile was generated from any information that is not publicly available, we treat the profile in the same way that we would treat the original data itself.

AVOIDING BIAS AND OVERFITTING ─────────

Even when data is clean and compliant, it is still susceptible to biases that can impact its validity. Earlier in the college campus shirt color example, we covered the different types of cognitive biases that can drive incorrect assumptions about people wearing red and blue shirts, including:

- Sampling errors

- Missing variables

- Social desirability

These biases can become embedded in any assessment or AI, causing misleading and undesirable results. While the bias baked into any Personality AI platform depends on the methods and standards of its developer, it is ultimately the end user's responsibility to use these insights in the proper way.

With Your Colleagues

Personality AI is most effective when it creates two-way value, and that makes it a powerful tool to help people collaborate and interact more effectively at work. With a Personality Map and a common language to describe behavior, two people can understand each other better, reconcile their differences, and learn how to deal with the other's strengths and blind spots.

However, people may use personality data to draw conclusions too early about another person, with too little data. This is called *overfitting*.

Overfitting a personality type is similar to stereotyping and may sound like this:

"I've worked with a Motivator before and we didn't get along, so I won't work with any other Motivators."

"The last Driver I worked with was fine with cursing at work, so I'll talk the same way with my new Driver manager."

"Stop being such an Analyst!"

Nobody wants to be painted with such a broad brush, and this kind of lazy thinking can lead to some very negative fallout—poor decisions, hurt feelings, and the compounding effect of building upon faulty assumptions over time.

This is why it is so important to (a) recognize DISC, the Personality Map, and other personality frameworks as a language to describe behavior, and (b) recognize Personality AI as a smart, but still imperfect, approach to understanding another person. Every insight that comes from Personality AI should be considered a "best guess" until it is either validated or invalidated by real world experience.

With Your Customers

Communication is only effective when the listener hears your message clearly. When you use Personality AI for sales or marketing outreach, this is the goal. It is a fundamentally empathetic and mutually beneficial value proposition.

However, the common concern among people who learn about Personality AI for the first time is that it could be used to coerce them into doing something that they actually do not want to do. It's easy to think of this kind of technology being adopted by a *1984*-style Big Brother and used for mass manipulation.

This is a concern that extends far beyond the scope of Personality AI, into the realm of social media, censorship, and artificial intelligence more broadly. And while you may understand the technical limitations and good intentions of your software tools, your customers may not.

Beyond complying with your country's data regulations, it's important to be able to explain the technologies and data you use to your customers. Here is a simple set of guidelines for Personality AI, specifically:

Personality AI Guidelines

- Make the source data and results available to customers upon request, rather than concealing information.

- Use personality insights for opening conversations and building long-term trust, rather than pushing someone to take an action for your short-term benefit.

- Use the most accurate possible method for detecting someone's personality with the tools available to you, rather than the most convenient method.

- State personality insights with the appropriate level of uncertainty, rather than treating every insight as fact without validation.

- Always treat people as the dynamic, complex individuals they are rather than oversimplified stereotypes or caricatures.

Chapter Twenty-Eight

RESTORING EMPATHY IN A HYPER-SKEPTICAL WORLD

We have discussed how the current versions of Personality AI can help you accelerate your career, strengthen existing relationships, and build new ones. We further covered how Personality AI can help you make better career decisions, communicate more effectively, build more productive teams, and be a better leader. However, we have barely scratched the surface of its applications outside the workplace.

As technology plays a larger and larger role in our lives, there will be more artificial barriers between people. This creates more obstacles to genuine connection and trusting relationships. We can't realistically face this challenge by removing technology; it's here to stay. But we can counteract technology's dehumanizing side effects by using new tools to understand each other better. While machines have at times removed human empathy from the equation in the name of efficiency, look to Personality AI as the machine that re-injects empathy into our communication channels.

Think about the world of possibilities in applying Personality AI to our personal relationships, such as dating, marriage, and family life. What if we all had a GPS for navigating these relationships just like our professional ones? Every human, at the core, has a desire to know others and be known by others. Abe Lincoln once wisely said, "I do not like that man. I must get to know him better." Many of our issues stem from a lack of understanding each other, and personality data can help us enjoy lives of more harmony and less destructive conflict. More connection and less miscommunication. More clicking and less clashing.

Because of the rise of personality profiles and the tools that make them accessible, it isn't that hard to picture this kind of world. Personality AI gives us the ability to create a new layer of empathy in the smaller worlds around us. Like our executive coach we mentioned earlier, Walt, we all now have the ability to understand others on a deeper level, much earlier in our relationships, and with a real road map for navigating our differences.

We now have the choice to move forward in our ignorance, or to make every interaction richer, more meaningful, and more effective with empathy.

ACKNOWLEDGMENTS

Although Greg and I were the ones who eventually put pen to paper, this book would not have been possible without the contributions of many more people who have supported, advised, and inspired us over the years. We are, in many ways, standing on the shoulders of giants, and we would like to acknowledge some of those people individually.

We must start with the ones who devoted much of their lives to give us the opportunity to pursue this strange, exciting entrepreneurial path in life. Our respective parents, Stuart and Joan Skloot, as well as Andy and Doreen D'Agostino, have made countless sacrifices over the years to lay strong foundations that we can build on today.

This book is largely a product of what we have learned since building and releasing Crystal, a software platform that thousands of organizations use today for personality assessments, personality predictions, and communication tools. In our company's first few years, a handful of brave people believed in the vision enough to join us in our risky, ambitious, unpredictable adventure. That small team helped bring our vision to life.

In those early days, we were also pushed forward by a supportive, wise group of partners and advisors. People like Jeremy Hitchcock, Krista Sheets, Richard Banfield, Dharmesh Shah, Christopher O'Donnell, Nicholas Holland, Sean Lindsay, Michael Wright, Todd Tyler, and John Barrows profoundly influenced our product, technology, and business. Others like Marc Benioff, John Somorjai, Matt Garrett, Rob Keith, Sean Ammirati, Dan Frawley, Brad Coffey, Kyle Porter, and Sean Kester provided key partnerships for our young company.

Acknowledgments

The psychological models that drive Crystal's Personality AI technology—the models at the heart of this book—are derived from hundreds of years of scientific study and clinical observation. We drew heavily upon the work of psychologists from the past, like Carl Jung and William Marston, as well as today's leading personality experts, like Colin DeYoung, Yanna Weisberg, and Lena Quilty. Their research is frequently cited throughout the book, and Personality AI would not be possible without it.

Throughout the entire process of writing the book, several individuals made enormous contributions to its content through painstaking research, revisions, and edits. These hardworking and meticulous souls include Brittney Julian, Walter Miltenberger, Megan Bandy, Carter Wright, Richard Narramore, and Vicki Adang.

Aside from those people we mentioned, hundreds of other friends, customers, investors, journalists, and partners have helped us make this happen. We feel a tremendous amount of gratitude toward each of them, and for the faith that they have put in us and our team.

ABOUT THE AUTHORS

Drew D'Agostino (https://www.crystalknows.com/) is the CEO of Crystal, the app that tells you anyone's personality. Using AI, Crystal accurately identifies a person's motivations, communication style, and other behavioral traits. Thousands of professionals globally use Crystal to communicate more effectively, write more persuasively, and build trust faster with new people. Previously, Drew was CTO of Attend.com, an event management software company. Drew and his company have been featured in *Inc.*, *Fortune*, *CNN*, *Fast Company*, *MIT Technology Review*, *Wired*, and *The Guardian*.

Greg Skloot (https://www.crystalknows.com/) is the president and COO of Crystal and a passionate evangelist for leveraging AI to better understand anyone's personality and build stronger relationships. Previously, Greg was vice president of growth at fitness-technology startup Netpulse, where he led sales, customer success, marketing, and operations until the company was acquired by eGym in 2018. Earlier, he was the CEO of Attend.com, an event management software company.

INDEX

Note: Page references in *italics* refer to figures and tables.

Index